INFORMATION TECHNOLOGY
A Revolutionary Change

INFORMATION TECHNOLOGY
A Revolutionary Change
(In 9 Volumes)

Volume 3
(Economic and Political Dimensions of Information Age)

Editor
RAMESH CHANDRA
Vice-Chancellor, Bundelkhand University, Jhansi (U.P.)

KALPAZ PUBLICATIONS
DELHI–110052

INFORMATION TECHNOLOGY: A REVOLUTIONARY CHANGE

(Information Technology)

Rs. 8000 (Set)
Rs. 900 (Each Volume)

ISBN: 81-7835-201-X (Set)
ISBN: 81-7835-222-2 (Vol. 3)

Published in 2003 in India by
Kalpaz Publications
C–30, Satyawati Nagar
Delhi–110052
E-mail: kalpaz@hotmail.com

Laser Typesetting at: Varsha Graphics, Delhi
Printed at: Mehra Offset Printers, New Delhi

Contents

Preface

The digital convergence of information and communication technologies (ICTs) has lessened two long-standing obstacles to communication delay and distance. Ever cheaper, ever more rapid, and ever more varied means of communicating vast amounts of information through the internet, among other networks, is creating a world in which there is far greater access to information than ever before.

The increasing economic importance of ICTs is linked to the growth of electronic commerce. An increasingly important part of all commercial activity on the digital market is geared toward the control over access to cyberspace. The gates that provide access to the World Wide Web have become crucial targets in the struggle for dominance in this market. The growth of electronic commerce initially raised concerns about implications for the labour market, but there is also the expectation that few jobs will really be lost since companies will continue to use traditional forms of commerce along with digital trading. When digital trading finally predominates, some jobs will be lost, but new ones requiring new skills will also have been created.

Many developing countries are in a good position to exploit the opportunities of the technology revolution and advance human development. Others face significant hurdles, lacking the kind of economic environment that encourages innovation, lacking the skills and institutions to adapt new technologies to local needs and constraints. But sound public policy can make a difference. The key is to create an environment that mobilizes people's creative potential to use and develop technological innovations.

The book argues that access to ICTs should not be seen as an end in itself; the measure of success remains progress towards reaching the international development targets, rather than the spread of technology or bridging the digital divide.

Editor

1
Introduction

The digital convergence of information and communication technologies (ICT) has lessened two long-standing obstacles to communication delay and distance. Ever cheaper, ever more rapid, and ever more varied means of communicating vast amounts of information through the Internet, among other networks, is creating a world in which there is far greater access to information than ever before. Is a "new economy" emerging? ICT is making access to information more "symmetrical" more people have access to more information whenever and wherever they need it and this is disrupting established economic relations.

The effect will be profound changes in the structure of markets and organizations and established patterns of economic behaviour. While much attention has surrounded the volatile new world of the "dot.coms", this is a distraction: the true portent of ICT is how it will transform the "old economy". Changes in how the economy works will transform the world of work. The creation and loss of jobs, the content and quality of work, the location of work, the nature of the employment contract, the skills required and how often they can be obtained, the organization of work and the functioning and effectiveness of worker and employer organizations all are affected by the emerging era of digital globalization. Knowledge workers, those who generate ideas and transmit these electronically as "intangible" or "immaterial" products, gain particular advantage in the networking economy: through the Internet and other networking technologies, they have access any time to unlimited amounts of the "raw material" of knowledge creation. Yet there is a knowledge component to all work, and the illiterate farmer can also gain from greater access to information. Nor does networking necessarily mean an increase in knowledge or skill requirements. Unskilled or de-skilled jobs skill polarization in the networking economy also exist.

ICT is a "meta-technology" characterized by pervasive effects on the economy as a whole, and on areas of scientific and technological advance well beyond the ICT sector itself. Barring a disaster scenario, the onrush of information itself is irreversible; however, its course is by no means pre-ordained or pre-determined. This will clearly be a "steerable revolution", in which wise policies and appropriate institutions will be essential toward directing change toward the greatest public good. Passivity will lead to marginalization. Periods of rapid technological change give rise to innovation and creativity, the outcomes of which cannot be known in advance. One effect of the technologies is clear: work is becoming independent of location and this will change management practices, the nature of the employment contract, and the quality of work. Also, the ability to organize production in "real time" anywhere in the world will no doubt induce changing patterns in the global division of labour. The digital era has diffused at an astonishing rate. Fifty million people were navigating the Internet within its first four years and their numbers are increasing at a rapid rate. But speed also means disruption and division.

Disruption occurs as the inadequacies of existing institutions and regulatory frameworks are exposed to rapid change and new demands. Institutions and organizations that do not adjust risk irrelevance. Technological change always favours the prepared: the world's different speeds of change and different stages of preparedness mean that the existing "digital divides" are certain to widen.

Within countries, the digital divide often has common characteristics. Use of the Internet, for example, is more common among younger than older people, men than women, the more rather than the less educated, urban rather than rural dwellers, and those with higher incomes. One, if not the most significant factor is the level of education, as education itself is related to income and often to location. Girls lag in educational attainment in most countries and, even in wealthy ones, their enrolment in the core courses of the technologies is a small share of boys' enrolment.

Between countries, the divide's features also have common characteristics. Barely 6 per cent of the world's people have ever logged onto the Internet and 85 to 90 per cent of them are in the industrialized countries. The level of national income is strongly related to ICT diffusion and is clearly the distinguishing feature of the divide between industrialized and developing countries. The cost and availability of telecommunications determines the extent to which the Internet is used, and per capita access costs are most often higher in poorer countries. Coercive governments limit the extent to which information is exchanged, and evidence shows a higher level of Internet usage where political and civil freedoms exist.

Macro-policies and features of the regulatory environment have a determining influence on the degree to which enterprises will adopt new technologies, how they will use them, and whether new enterprises will be created. In general terms, however, it is the incentives that the technologies create at the micro-level and the strong pressure of competition B that will directly determine the economic and employment effects of ICT. Using ICT lowers costs and can increase productivity economy-wide, including in "old economy" industries. As costs are lowered throughout the economy, some believe that a "new economy" will emerge one characterized by a higher level of potential growth consistent with low inflation.

The most that can be said at present is the appearance of a few hopeful signs surrounding the changing price relations associated with ICT. Available evidence does show that electronic markets are more transparent and, through lower transaction costs, appear to result in substantial changes in established price relations. For example, some evidence shows that electronic markets can result in up to 15 per cent lower costs for consumers. It is far more significant that lower costs are also apparent in inter-enterprise or "B2B" transactions across many "old economy" industries. The ICT sector itself is the fastest-growing sector in many industrialized countries. Although the ICT sector usually does not account for much more than 5 per cent of the workforce in any OECD country, the sector's contribution to GDP growth is disproportionately great.

Globalization had already spurred an internal transformation of the enterprise, resulting in changes in the organization of work toward flatter hierarchies and project-based teams. The need for a more rapid response to volatile product markets and declining product life cycles has also been behind the trend toward greater outsourcing. The emerging era of "digital globalization" is accelerating these organizational changes.

Enterprises in the most globally competitive industries have experienced both a decline in the time devoted to strategy formulation and a qualitative change in the nature of competitive advantage. "time-to-market" has arisen as a critical competitive asset. This in turn compels companies to rely on the creativity, knowledge, and ability to acquire new knowledge of their core employees. Evidence shows that major gains in enterprise performance only occur where the use of the new technologies has been combined with wide-ranging changes in work organization.

Evidence also shows that the most widespread use of the new technologies exists in enterprises that have adopted the most thorough range of work organization changes, such as the decentralization of decision-making, and the organization of work into semi-autonomous, task-oriented teams.

The fast pace of competition means that, for some highly skilled activities, companies are relying on the external labour market for inputs of temporary duration. The technologies, meanwhile, allow companies to source work independently of location.

The outsourcing of needed inputs is accelerated both by the enabling technologies, as well as by competitive pressures. Locations (in both industrialized and developing countries) that have the adequate infrastructure and skills in their labour markets can benefit by participation in new global value chains, in "intangible" product markets such as software development or data processing.

The convergence of "carrier" and "content" industries has resulted in mergers between large firms. At the same time, there are lower barriers to entry in a period of rapidly evolving technologies, in which creativity and innovation matter more than physical plant, physical raw materials, and investment capital. Business start-ups are on the rise.

A world economy integrated in real time carries with it both advantages and new sources of instability. For example, the fortunes of Internet firms and the remuneration of at least some of their workers are unusually dependent on volatile equity markets.

Capital markets, meanwhile the most integrated global markets of all through ICT have already proven their ability in recent years to be contributing sources of massive job destruction. It is also true that value chains integrated in real time create dependencies that, in turn, increase vulnerability to disruption at any stage in the chain.

On the one hand, this could prove destabilizing as natural or human-made disturbances anywhere at any one point in a highly integrated chain could have immediate repercussions elsewhere. On the other, another effect of this could well be to increase the leverage that workers and their organizations could bring to bear on the enterprise that employs them. Finally, a higher level of integration between some developing country locations and industrialized countries could increase the relative exclusion of locations that are not connected. This is another reason why appropriate policies at both international and national levels - involving both the public and private sectors - will be necessary for increasing the gains arising from the use of the technologies.

Guardedly optimistic on the chances for employment growth where ICT is most in use. Productivity growth is greatest in the core ICT sector itself, where, in manufacturing it has resulted in stunning increases in output with nevertheless declining employment. But the employment decline in manufacturing has been more than offset by the rapid growth of new markets and new employment in the service sector, with business and producer services and social services (health, education) claiming the highest share of growth.

In France, for example, evidence shows that the negative effects of labour-saving investments in ICT in manufacturing have been largely compensated by job growth in services, business services in particular. Evidence shows that the countries that have had the greatest growth in "total factor productivity" in the 1990s are those where ICT has been used most widely in the economy.

These are also the countries in which employment has grown the most. There is evidence that employment ratios are highest in those countries where the use of ICT is most widespread. Evidence also shows that unemployment has declined most in the small number of countries where Internet use is most widespread, such as Denmark, Finland and Ireland. It is too early to conclude, but there are hopeful signs that the effect of ICT on employment is positive.

Use of the technologies is nevertheless associated with new patterns of job creation and job loss. And despite the hopeful signs of employment creation, it is clear that jobs will also be lost through three main channels obsolescence, automation, and "disintermediation".

ICT replaces old tasks and occupations through automation, such as the telephone switchboard operator. But the technologies also create new tasks and occupations, such as Webpage designers or call-centre workers or a variety of new intermediaries. Consensus reigns on the fact that the highest rates of job creation, job destruction, and job switching occur among the most technologically innovative firms in sectors where overall employment is growing. More generally, ICT creates jobs for occupations in rising demand, such as software programmers, while destroys jobs in those skills in declining demand, such as those associated with analog technologies.

Since ICT enables routine tasks to be "codified" and automated as part of the labour-saving increases in productivity that arise with the use of ICT B this, of course, is a source of job loss. Some jobs based on information intermediation travel agents, for example could be lost through more direct access to information or change in function. Through the Internet and email, when work is independent of location, new ways of working arise. There has been a rise in self-employment.

A growing number of "e-lancers" move from enterprise to enterprise or project to project on their own, sometimes for months, sometimes for days.

In labour markets that are at the forefront of the digital economy, such as Silicon Valley, the share of self-employed and temporary workers is far higher than the national average. The skill levels and value to the firm of these individuals are high, but the firm specificity of their knowledge is low. In consequence, diversity is increasing in those labour markets where ICT has diffused the most. Although disaggregated data are unavailable, the share of self-employed, temporary and part-time work has been rising in most OECD countries.

The margin of the digital workforce that is mobile has needs that both the reform of existing labour market institutions and the growth of new ones can address. Both public and private employment agencies are extending their range of services beyond the job-matching function to the additional needs of a mobile workforce. While there is substantial variety in the agency work industry, the most advanced companies are not only major providers of career continuity for their temporary workforce, but also providers of skills as well. Trade unions and employer organizations are also offering services to these new independent workers.

The theory that labour markets in the digital era are undergoing profound transformation has some basis in truth. For most people at work, however, there continues to be a surprisingly high degree of employment stability. In 12 out of 16 OECD countries' labour markets examined, "job tenure", a measure of employment stability, has either remained unchanged during the last decade of the 1990s, or had in fact increased. Even looking more closely at some of the occupations most associated with the "new economy", such as telecommunications workers or those in the distribution sector, job tenure has remained largely unchanged.

Continued employment stability despite an era of fast-paced technological change is not an unreasonable expectation for at least two reasons. First, and as noted earlier, the OECD labour market is ageing. Job tenure always increases with the age of the workforce.

A second reason may relate to how ICT and globalization are affecting competitive advantage. As "time-to-market" becomes increasingly important, the organization of work needs to adjust so that a high degree of creativity and a more rapid response to product market pressures can occur. Critical to the new organization of work is the increased need to "tap" the tacit knowledge of the workforce. To do so requires a workplace culture in which trust and experimentation can simultaneously occur. Such behaviours are unlikely to occur between relative strangers in workplaces characterized by a high degree of instability and frequent turnover.

Employment stability is no indication of the absence of change. Labour markets have indeed become more demanding, more diversified, and more turbulent. But most of this turbulence is being internalized with the enterprise, where jobs are indeed changing. Nor does employment stability mean employment security: contracts are changing, stress is on the rise, cites evidence of employment insecurity perceived by workers up and down the organizational hierarchy.

The considerable emphasis on the independence of work from any physical location. This is a feature of teleworking from home, but it also refers to the relocation of jobs from industrialized to developing countries, such as "back-office" staff located in call centres, data entry and processing, software development. Work that is independent of location has a growing share of employment in industrialized countries. For example, almost one-fourth of the workforce in the United Kingdom now carries out at least some of its work at home. By 2003, there will be an estimated 1.3 million employed in call centres in the European Union, up from an estimated 670,000 in 2001. Women are often thought to benefit from the new independence of work location.

In some ways, this is clearly the case: working from home, for example, can allow a better accommodation of work and family schedules. But isolation and exclusion from career choices can also occur. Women tend less than men to mix telework with stays at the office. Nor is women's telework as mobile as men's, but concentrated at home. At home, women are more likely to combine telework with family responsibilities, whereas men are more likely to separate the two. Call centres and data processing in developing countries are predominantly female occupations. But data processing, although it may be better than other local labour market alternatives, may not lead to career upgrading. And wages and conditions of work in call centres appear to vary widely. In the best, a new, more informal and more appealing work culture may be apparent; but, in the worst instances, call centres have been called the "sweatshops of the digital era".

One estimate suggests that up to 5 per cent of all service-sector jobs in industrialized countries could be "contestable" by developing countries. This would amount to about 12 million jobs in which relocation to developing countries could occur. For example, in the

Caribbean countries, almost 5,000 women were employed in data processing activities in the late 1990s. Such jobs can provide developing countries with an important toehold in global export markets, as well as providing direct employment and foreign exchange earnings. But if the magnitude of the relocation of work is a credible estimate, it implies that the greatest employment potential of ICT for developing countries needs to lie elsewhere.

Beyond participation in global value chains through the increasing tradability of services, the technologies offer the chance for purely domestic activities and associated job growth. Through telecentres, for example, countries such as Bangladesh, India and Senegal and others have been able to create direct employment for thousands of women and men. Over the last four years in India, for example, an estimated 250,000 jobs for women have been created through mobile telephony centres. Such local entrepreneurial activities are likely to have positive externalities on local economies as well. Evidence also shows that women's operation of telecentres increases the participation of women as consumers of these services.

It is clear that ICT is merely a tool, and tools do not substitute for genuine development. ICT, however, offer tools that may accelerate development. Since the principal consequence of ICT is greater access to and use of information, it is precisely those locations that have the least of both where the technologies could have the greatest marginal impact.

Telecommunications are positively correlated with economic growth. Even mobile telephony can be a stimulus to local economic development and, in causal terms, some evidence shows that better telecommunications are likely to be a source of economic growth.

A widening digital divide may be inevitable, but using the technologies can be beneficial at any level of economic development. The potential welfare gains for developing countries are of three major types.

— Countries with the right mix of skills, infrastructure, and policies could become important locations in global markets for intangible products or ICT products generally. Countries as diverse as Brazil, China, Costa Rica, Israel, Malaysia and Romania have all been able to gain niches in such markets. Some commonalities underlie their success. It is clear, for example, that for maximum gains to emerge, the development of essential ICT skills, including software development, is necessary. Without such skills, the technologies can neither be maintained nor adapted to local usages, from which greater economic advantages are obtained.

— Acceleration of development can occur through the leapfrogging potentials inherent in the technologies, where leapfrogging is defined as the ability to bypass earlier investments in the time or cost of development. Leapfrogging has first of all a technological foundation: through wireless applications, developing countries can bypass more costly and time-consuming investments in fixed-wire telecom infrastructures. In economic terms, leapfrogging can occur through several channels. For example, developing countries have often gained an initial niche in export markets through comparative advantage in cheap, unskilled labour, as is characteristic of the garment industry. Where appropriate skills are available, countries can now bypass this earlier, lower value-added entrance into global markets in favour of greater value-added production. An example is Costa Rica, where the educational level of the workforce was a vital factor in Intel's decision to locate a semiconductor production facility. Small enterprises in developing countries have at least potential access to a global market for both tangible and intangible products. For example, pockets of software development are now occurring in the Philippines and in Viet Nam for clients identified through the Internet. For tangible products, provided that the physical infrastructure is adequate enough for the fulfilment of transactions to occur, countries can find markets for goods in which they have an unassailable competitive advantage, such as products made locally or cultural artefacts. In many cases, leapfrogging refers to advantages at the microeconomic level. For macroeconomic gains to occur requires a range of commercial, trade, investment, telecommunications and other infrastructure policies to be brought to bear on the development potential of ICT. China's strategy is particularly promising in this regard. It has combined previously separate ministries into the Ministry of Information Industries, and established economic zones particularly devoted to the growth of start-up ICT ventures

— Underpin a new development paradigm arises from the possibilities that networking opens up for poverty alleviation. To the extent that ICT can improve aggregate economic growth, this could generate linkages to activities that provide livelihoods for those who are poor. Poor people could also benefit directly through access to the information that the technologies provide or through the potential for greater collective voice and empowerment they allow.

— To the extent that the technologies can make governments more transparent, extend their services more broadly, and at lower cost, the poor could benefit from the improved quality and reach of health, education and social services. This could also create opportunities for women through access to learning, incomes, and greater autonomy. Access to ICT for poor segments of the population is likeliest to occur at the community level. A key focus for expanding such access could be through the improvement of NGO capacities and other local development agencies in, for example, the fields of health care, child welfare, or basic education or nutrition.

Need of ICT Education

Literacy and education cannot be leapfrogged, yet both are vital for reaping the greatest advantages from the emerging digital era. The promotion of education and literacy generally, and digital literacy in particular, is a challenge facing all countries. Educational differences underlie the different rates of penetration of ICT and Internet usage. For example, the ICT world is often depicted as a world of relatively young men, and the available evidence supports this depiction. Two-thirds of the world's illiterate are girls and women. Nor are girls sufficiently enrolled in the science curricula at the core of the technologies' innovation and use. In the wealthiest countries, substantial progress has been made in ensuring access to the Internet in schoolrooms.

The European Union's programme, for example, is for 100 per cent "connectivity" in schools by the end of 2001. Access alone is insufficient: teachers need to be trained in the substance of the new technologies and their most effective use.

Even in the wealthiest countries, such training is far from thorough, and investments in the pursuit of this objective are often minimal. Obviously, for the majority of the world's people, this objective is distant from reality. In the poorest countries, the main objectives need to continue to be the promotion of literacy and access to general education. Poorly equipped schools or their absence altogether are most characteristic of the poorest locations.

Through their application to distance-learning, the technologies could greatly multiply access to learning opportunities for those who most need them. Distance learning applications, while costly to develop, have low unit costs the more there are people who use them. In such locations, distance learning can be an important complement to existing education providers.

Wealth creation in the wealthiest countries relies less on physical inputs than on knowledge. The frontiers of knowledge itself, however, are rapidly expanding. Two consequences of this are, first, a shift in teaching methodologies away from the transfer of facts to students as passive recipients, and, instead, towards teaching students how to learn and instilling in them the curiosity to do so. In short, how people learn is becoming as important as what they learn.

A parallel trend is observable in high tech firms exposed to fast-paced competition. The ability to learn, to transform existing knowledge into new knowledge, is a source of competitive advantage of increasing significance. In such companies, daily learning has become an integral part of the job. Part of such learning relies on the exchange of tacit knowledge among employees.

The adoption of ICT in enterprises is creating two types of skill needs. The first relates to a variety of foundation skills, such as the ability to learn, to communicate, and to analyse and solve problems, all of which are essential to work environments that rely on rapid innovation, and the interpersonal exchange and creation of knowledge. Beyond such skills, however, are the technical skills related to ICT itself, the need for which extends well beyond the ICT sector to the economy as a whole.

Where the technologies are most broadly in use, skill shortages particularly in the technical support skills surrounding both hardware and software applications are acute, if difficult to quantify. This, in turn, is a brake on economic growth for enterprises that would otherwise adopt the technologies' applications more readily. Three problems relating to the skills shortage are of particular significance. The first of these is the debate over labour migration. The availability of technical skills in developing countries could be used to meet the skill needs of industrialized countries.

On the positive side, migrant workers benefit from the greater experience and higher wages that migration can bring, and sending countries can benefit from the remittances their expatriates send home. It is also true that countries such as China, India and Viet Nam have all benefited from the networks their expatriates have created outside the country, and also from the skills and experiences they repatriate when they do return home. For receiving countries, of course, reliance on foreign labour is a way of overcoming skill shortages in the short term.

On the negative side, however, the outward migration of the technically skilled can result in a brain drain, depriving developing countries of these scarce skills. For example, possibly all of India's annual graduates in ICT-related core skills could be in demand in industrialized countries. For receiving countries, meanwhile, there are two problems. First, some evidence suggests that the attractiveness of skilled migrant labour in the United States comes from the lower pay that employers can offer them relative to domestic labour.

Additionally, there is concern in both the United States as well as in European Union countries that recourse to foreign labour might detract from the need for the training and retraining of the existing workforce. This is particularly the case where emerging skill shortages coexist with still relatively high unemployment. A second and related problem is the ageing workforce in many OECD countries. This implies, first of all, that the majority of "tomorrow's workforce" is, in fact, already on the job.

The promotion of lifelong learning and the retraining of the existing workforce need therefore to be policy objectives applied to those already at work. Equipping workers with ICT-related skills, therefore, will need to be specifically targeted to the needs of older workers. A third problem is the possibility of a skills polarization emerging as the technologies are taken up by enterprises.

On the high end, highly skilled workers using ICT-related skills intensively on the job may have broad career options and command high salaries. But there remain many jobs in the networking economy that are low-skilled and low-paid. The polarization of skills could also reinforce the gender-based segmentation of the labour market.

There are many avenues available to address the greater need for retraining and lifelong learning. Both feature prominently in enterprise training policies, as well as in the strategies of trade unions, and access to learning opportunities increasingly features in national tripartite agreements or at the collective bargaining table. In Singapore, for example, the Critical Enabling Skills Training (CREST) programme will enrol 100,000 trainees in 2001.

Germany's tripartite Alliance for Jobs agreed on the creation of training places for 60,000 people in ICT up to 2003. In South Africa, a tripartite training authority in the ICT sector specifically was set up in 2000. Addressing the skills shortage has resulted in new ways in which training is delivered and new deliverers of that training. Distance-learning is a valuable substitute for classroom instruction.

For example, multinational enterprises are increasingly using distance learning applications for their staff worldwide: in an environment of rapid change, lifelong learning has become critical to corporate success, as well as to the employability of workers. Classrooms are a poor substitute for learning vehicles that can be used anywhere, anytime, such as distance-learning. Evidence also suggests that interactive, multimedia formats can often be a more effective means of knowledge retention than classroom lectures. To remedy a worldwide shortage of skills in ICT makes good economic sense and will require both an innovative new range of public/private partnerships as well as investments of human and financial resources.

The networking economy offers genuine potential for striking a better balance between work and family responsibilities, or work and leisure. Work itself has become more rewarding for many in its pay and in its content. The creation and use of knowledge on the job can be inherently more satisfying than the monotony of narrow tasks performed under strict supervision. The independence of work from its location can be liberating not only in spatial terms, but also in the ability to schedule work when desired.

The increasing knowledge content of work should favour the equality of women and men in the workforce. Intelligence and creativity are also homogeneously distributed between industrialized and developing countries, or between people with and without physical disabilities. The digital era's potential to improve the quality of work and life is clearly real. But it is not a given.

The values, agreements, and institutions of an earlier industrial era are often no longer suited to current trends in working conditions. Gaps in social protection are opening up. Some of the self-employed, for example, are in disguised self-employment, dependent on an individual employer but without the benefits of an employment contract. Also, as stimulating as work can be in fast-paced, semi-autonomous work teams, not all workers are likely to appreciate the greater risks associated with greater responsibility. These risks extend from the need to keep oneself "employable" through continuous learning to the greater stress of having simultaneously to manage competing demands, cope with information "overload", etc.

An irony of the communications revolution, moreover, is that a sharply higher intensity of virtual communications can go hand in hand with increased isolation. That much work in the digital era can be done anywhere, anytime has meant for some that this is precisely what is occurring, with a consequent blurring of hours or work and hours of leisure. Far from adjusting working needs to the needs of family life, there can be rising pressure to work everywhere and all the time.

Older workers could be excluded from the new careers and opportunities created by the technologies, and women, too, as they lag behind men in scientific and technical training. The highlights many more risks, ranging from those of health and safety, to invasions of privacy, and skill polarization.

Addressing the negative consequences of changes in the nature of work has been the key function of industrial relations. In creating a more diversified labour market, however, the diffusion of these technologies renders the effort of collective organization and representation far more difficult. The technologies are associated with smaller units of production and they accelerate both the trend toward outsourcing, as well as the frequent redefinition of who is a core employee and who is not. Fragmentation in the organization of production, and a continually changing organization of work, are additional challenges to organizing workers in the new economy.

The effects of ICT on the quality of life at work have strong potentials in both positive and negative directions. It is clear that the need for worker protection remains and is arguably greater in the context of the disruptive changes that are occurring.

There is evidence of the need for changing attitudes and strategies within the trade union movement to address issues of organizing and the representation of new areas of worker protection. Some international trade secretariats, such as the Union Network International (UNI), have comprehensive strategies and programmes in place for the networking economy. For example, UNI's "online rights for online workers" campaign emphasizes employee representatives' right to corporate email and intranet communications, and the right for privacy and due process in the monitoring of employee communications. Various of the risks to the quality of life at work are also being addressed by trade unions in their policies, bargaining agreements, or tripartite negotiations.

Of these, the right to lifelong learning and access to such opportunities is perhaps the most fundamental, and one where substantial progress is being made. In recognition of the fact that teleworking creates welcome opportunities for some employees but also risks it, too, is an area in which collective bargaining is extensive. Common features in telework agreements include that it be undertaken voluntarily, that the worker's decision is reversible, and that the pay and employment status of the teleworker are not downgraded. The issue of stress at the workplace is also beginning to enter the bargaining agendas of trade unions.

The digital reproduction of intellectual property is a concern of workers in the entertainment and media interests, and a focus of bargaining for journalists. Trade unions are also addressing the digital divide through expanding access to the new technologies. Both the Swedish LO and the AFL-CIO in the United States, for example, assist in the effort to overcome the within-country digital divide through the provision of low-cost, Internet-connected PCs to members.

International trade secretariats are also assisting their affiliates in developing countries to become digitally literate. However much it may be the case that the present era of technological change presents certain risks to labour market institutions, the technologies can also be of benefit to trade unions and employer organizations. For example, some employer organizations, such as ALMEGA in Sweden, have created an online presence a "virtual employers' organization" allowing them to provide interactive services, individually tailored to members' interests. The Web allows them to reach out to non-members as well, particularly the new small firms in the new economy.

For trade unions, the fundamental aim remains that of organizing the new, more diverse ICT workforce. UNI has targeted the organizing of freelance workers as a priority area, for example. Some trade unions have established organizations especially for the self-employed.

In the Netherlands, the Allied Union in the FNV federation created the FNV Zelfstandige Bondgenoten in 1999, the first Dutch trade union specifically for self-employed people. In the United States, a variant of the "guild model" of organization is being experimented with by a newly formed organization affiliated to the Communication Workers of America: the Washington Alliance of Technology Workers (WashTech) is a new Web-based service provider for agency and directly employed workers in the ICT sector, offering individual services, rather than collective bargaining. Access to information and the collective strength of communication can assist trade unions in redressing imbalances of power in the workplace.

The Internet was the vehicle through which the Seattle protests against the World Trade Organization meeting in 1999 were organized. There are also numerous examples of how the Internet has been used to increase the "symmetry of information" at the bargaining table. Through the Internet, local disputes can "go global". Many trade unions have engaged in "cyber-pickets" to shed light broadly on violations of worker rights and bad industrial relations practices. In a global organization of production that increasingly relies on information flows in real time, giving greater leverage to the voice of workers is a clear possibility.

The issue of policies needed to increase the potential gains of the emerging digital era and lessen the costs of adjustment. The positive potential of the technologies for employment growth, a better quality of life, and as a tool for reinforcing the development agenda is beyond doubt. Not beyond doubt is whether this potential can be translated into reality for the majority of the world's people anytime soon - or whether the risks of change can be avoided.

2

E-Commerce

E-commerce has led to profound changes in the way business is conducted. Networked organizations and decentralized corporate processes have changed relationships between the producers and users of goods and services, and spurred the rapid integration of global markets. Information and communication technologies and new developments such as online business-to-business exchanges and virtual trading networks have transformed traditional business practices by connecting critical business systems directly to key constituents like customers, employees, suppliers and distributors via the Internet. These exchanges have reshaped the world of business and trade transactions. The private sector has been the driving force behind this phenomenon. The paradox remains, however, that while networked technologies are a great leveler of economic and social structures, they also have the potential to exacerbate the "digital divide" —the gap between the level of e-commerce development in industrial countries and that in countries and organizations standing on the sidelines of the global e-commerce revolution.

Internet-based business-to-business electronic commerce creates new market structures that enable business partners to switch allegiances at low cost, since the Internet expands choices and options to suppliers and consumers on an exponential basis. In addition, it enables contracting parties to exchange information, best practices and market feedback in real time. Countries left out of the loop could experience the costs of severe economic isolation in this highly competitive environment. Recent findings by Computer Economics, an e-business adviser to corporations, suggest that while e-commerce will continue to boom in the next decade, Africa, South America and parts of Asia could be left out of the trade revolution.

There is a very real possibility that developing countries may be constantly playing catch-up with the technologies and policy principles that have been formulated in the developed world. Also, the "digital divide" is hampering the ability of developing economies to be part of the ongoing process in developed economies: of assessing and possibly re-defining the existing rules for global electronic commerce.

One of the key functions of the Global Information Infrastructure Commission (GIIC), an independent, non-governmental initiative launched during the G-7 summit meeting at Brussels in 1995, has been to ensure that developing countries are constantly engaged in this dialogue.

Through its global network of private and public sector commissioners who represent both developed and developing countries, the GIIC has worked with national governments, industry groups, and international organizations - to advance the dialogue on the rules needed for the global information economy, as well as to create awareness and build constituencies for change. In its work over the past five years, several factors have led the GIIC to conclude that the global networked economy needs increasingly flexible legislative solutions to the challenges posed by rapid technological change. The factors are:

1. Regulatory Frameworks in Constant Flux

The technological convergence of telecommunications and computers has revolutionized the way in which society produces, stores, and uses information. Meanwhile, the rapid growth of networks across national boundaries has blurred the lines between providers, suppliers, and originators of information.These developments have called into question how regulatory systems can ensure trust, confidence and consumer protection within a rapidly globalizing technological environment.

For example, on-line issues related to digital copying and Internet domain names are raising critical issues about the ownership of copyrights and patents - and are creating brief and sometimes fluctuating values for intellectual property rights, privacy, and security, as information is digitally transformed and moves through its various iterations.

The continued education of government regulators and consumers, as well as the development of technology-neutral self-regulatory schemes in partnership with the private sector, is essential to spur institutional adaptation and quick response to new technologies and applications.

2. New Definitions of Individual Rights

In networked economy, businesses can employ data integration technologies such as customer profiling to understand customer needs, provide support over the Internet, and integrate these customer demands within their supply chain. The use of these technologies is leading to increased awareness of what consumers perceive as potential violations of their rights as individuals, such as the misuse or usurpation of personal data, inaccurate and incomplete information and payment fraud. By the same token, the networked economy has put information and power back into the hands of the individual, with user communities being redefined in accordance with common interests rather than by geographical or physical proximity.

In the electronic age, the buyer has access to information - and is thus empowered to change loyalty in an instant. So if businesses in the electronic age are to maintain customer loyalty and be competitive, they have to improve the service and value they bring to their customers. Businesses recognize that it is in their best interests to protect the privacy of their customers, and to build trust and confidence that personal data are accurate and will not be misused.

As a result, businesses are collaborating to develop self-regulatory codes of conduct, trustmarks, and seals to ensure flexible yet enforceable trust systems that are awarded to online retailers who comply with a high- and independently verifiable standard for electronic commerce.

These seals cover every aspect of their operations, from their trading status to their privacy and security policy, customer service and support policy, information integrity, and warranty information. In its work in both developing and developed countries, the GIIC has observed that many countries do not have laws or cultural morés that support the preservation of personal privacy.

3. Challenges to Jurisdiction in Cyberspace

As transactions become more global, the control of government institutions over economic or other activity occurring in cyberspace is increasingly eroded. Jurisdiction and rules of origin are the two key factors impacting cross-border e-commerce, requiring that national and international frameworks be harmonized to enable dispute resolution and redress.

Currently, issues relating to taxation, intellectual property, and consumer protection all depend on the rules of origin -or country of consumption. However, as transactions move online and become increasingly global, both business and consumers are becoming wary of the costs they may incur if they need to engage in cross-border litigation of their rights.

By using Alternate Dispute Resolution (ADR), consumers and merchants can settle their disputes through a trusted third party in a low-cost and speedy way. There are several examples of ADR, such as BBBOnLine, part of the Council of Better Business Bureaus in the United States, and Cybertribunal in Canada.

Other organizations involved in international dispute settlement for electronic commerce are the ICC International Court of Arbitration of the International

Chamber of Commerce (ICC), and the World Intellectual Property Organization's Internet-based WIPO-Net, which has been set up to arbitrate IP-related electronic commerce issues. However, to give businesses and consumers in global electronic commerce additional certainty, together with robust, reliable electronic commerce transactions, such certification efforts need to be extended to other countries and jurisdictions.

4. Authentication and Security

Authentication and security are critical for assuring people that they are transacting electronic commerce in an environment free from illegal attack or trespass. Strong, market-led encryption technologies are essential, as well as minimum necessary legal frameworks to authenticate electronic signatures.

In addition, a legal framework must be in place to punish the dishonest. Since the private sector is leading in the area of encryption, there needs to be a partnership between the private sector and governments to create the frameworks necessary to ensure the trust and authentication needed to stem criminal activity.

Since users tend to distrust government controls on encryption, governments should commit to removing all controls on cryptographic technologies and applications and should cooperate with businesses to facilitate the internationally secure exchange of information.

5. Universal Commercial Codes

Legal codes specifying commercial, contractual, and liability issues are the underpinnings of electronic commerce and are essential to building consumer confidence. As global electronic commerce expands, businesses are looking to a permanent framework for electronic commerce transactions that is also guaranteed and recognized by national governments.

The 1996 Model Law of the United Nations Commission on International Trade Law (UNCITRAL) provides national legislators a technology-neutral framework of internationally acceptable rules to remove legal obstacles to e-commerce and creates a more secure legal electronic environment.

The Model Law has been the basis for the development of e-commerce laws in Singapore, Korea, and Colombia, and has spurred the discussion of similar initiatives in Australia, Canada, Chile, France, Hong Kong, India, Slovenia, Brazil, Mexico, Morocco, New Zealand, Peru, the Philippines, Thailand and Tunisia.

However, in spite of this activity, most countries have been slow to convert what has been the norm for commerce between parties for several centuries -- the exchange of paper documents -- into the electronic environment. Increased education and the involvement of the legal community within countries or trading blocs or regions such as Asia-Pacific Economic Cooperation and Free Trade Area of the Americas are critical to the rapid expansion of global electronic commerce and the involvement of additional countries.

The GIIC has been spurring the dialogue about removing barriers to electronic commerce in many countries around the world, including India, China, the Philippines and Venezuela, as well as many countries in Africa. In addition, the GIIC has worked in partnership with the Alliance of Global Business (AGB), a coalition of businesses in 140 countries, to urge governments to rely on business self-regulation and the voluntary use of empowering technologies to create trust across the spectrum of users and providers for e-commerce goods and services. Some initiatives include the AGB's 1999 Global Action Plan for Electronic Commerce, the Fact Sheet on the Duty-Free Treatment of Electronic Transmissions, and the Discussion Paper on Trade-Related Aspects of Electronic Commerce.

Most countries of the world are still only learning how various information technology innovations will affect the economy and labor markets. For developing countries, this process is far more profound, as governments and private sector groups endeavor to restructure their economies for the global digital economy. The G-8 representatives at the Okinawa summit have a unique and unprecedented opportunity to facilitate international cooperation for a secure global environment and a new international approach to building a global information economy in which every nation and every individual has a chance to participate. Any global approach or framework needs to be flexible enough to support the growth of the information economy, encourage trade and investment flows, create jobs, and provide consumers with the benefits of competition, while encouraging a stable, secure environment for electronic transactions.

Partnership with the private sector and international organizations such as World Intellectual Property Organization, the World Trade Organization, Organization for Economic Cooperation and Development and UNCITRAL is essential in creating cooperative systems to:

1. Exchange information about best practices.
2. Increase consumer satisfaction and confidence in doing business on the Internet.
3. Establish merchant credibility and trustworthiness.
4.. Support and enhance the self-regulation of Internet commerce.
5. Encourage the development of guidelines and symbols to support electronic commerce.

Countries need to extend these endeavors to provide technical and financial assistance to those nations on the sidelines of the global electronic commerce revolution and also to bring consumers and small and medium-sized enterprises in the dialogue. The inclusion of these actors can only serve to create a robust, secure, global information infrastructure, expand global trade and economic growth, and, most significantly, minimize the threat of an ever-widening digital divide.

Consumer Protection in Electronic Commerce

The study of consumer shopping makes a number of recommendactions that will focus the energies of policy-makers, providing evidence that there are certain key consumer protection issues that must be addressed. Many specific recommendations arise from the detailed research findings.

1. If consumers are to take full advantage of the global shopping mall theoretically offered by the internet, they must feel confident of receiving a consistent standard of consumer protection wherever they shop In order to make this possible, a co-ordinated

international approach is needed to the formulation of guidelines governing electronic commerce. National governments should be encouraged to adopt best practice guidelines developed at international level.

2. Because adherence to many aspects of best practice guidelines is voluntary, consumers need a way of recognising internet shops which offer high standards of consumer protection with ease, wherever in the world those shops are based. The development of an internationally recognised certification or labelling scheme, which indicates that shops meet agreed minimum standards on a range of key issues, would go a longway to offering this international reassurance.

3. As online consumers experience many types of problem, such as nondelivery of goods or obstruction in obtaining refunds, so there is a need for a third-party redress mechanism that offers a further channel to the consumer retailer that offers a furtherchannel to the consumer once dead lock has been reached with the retailer. Such a mechanism needs to cover all companies selling goods to consumers on the internet. It needs to be accessible, affordable, fast, consumer-friendly, and binding on the company concerned. For such a mechanism to have teeth regardless of where a consumer shops, it must be supported by national governments.

Consumers should be made aware of the full name of the company they are dealing with, as this may not always be the same as the web address. The Consumers must at least be provided with the retailer's geographic address, the country the company is registered in, a phone number, and an e-mail address. Where applicable, the consumer should also be given the registration number or licence number for the retailer, and contact information for the body with which the business is registered or authorised, to enable the consumer to check legitimacy. Sites should make it clear to the consumer which countries they deliver to, before the order process is embarked upon. This information should be clearly sign posted from the home page, and should be kept up to date. Sites must display one overall total price to the consumer before the order is completed, which should include any delivery charges. If sites are marketing to consumers in other countries, it is important that they design their sites with the facility to incorporate the delivery charge in the total price, once the consumer has provided the relevant information about where they live and what form of delivery they want.

Delivery charges can make a significant difference to the overall cost, so it is not acceptable to ask the customer to contact the retailer separately to obtain delivery costs. Retailers supplying to other countries can also do much more to assist consumers in converting prices into their own currencies. Only one in four of the sites in other countries purchased from gave any assistance with converting prices. This is not a difficult facility to provide, and helps the consumer considerably when deciding whether to make a purchase.

Terms and conditions contain essential information such as cancellation and cooling-off rights, payment and delivery terms, and dispute resolution, so it is essential that they be presented to the consumer before the purchase is completed. Retailers should design sites to ensure that purchasers are shown the terms and conditions before confirming their order, or are offered a link to click on to the terms and conditions before confirmation.

Terms and conditions must be clearly sign posted/ titled, and clearly differentiated from other information, so that consumers can identify that this is the legal part of the contract. Terms and conditions should be provided in a manner that can be readily printed off and kept by the consumer for future reference.

Consumers International and other consumer groups are firmly of the belief that the law governing internet transactions should be the law of the consumer's home country, in order that he or she is familiar with the protection available. This is a controversial area which is engendering much debate at present.

Some retailers do stipulate within the contract which law they would like to apply, but a final decision on this, should a dispute arise, will be taken by the judge hearing the case. If a retailer specifies that the law governing transactions on its site is that of the retailer's own country, rather than the consumer's country of residence, that condition must behighlighted to the consumer in a clear and unambiguous manner.

If a consumer agrees to such a contract, the consumer must not be deprived of the key consumer protections offered in his/her own country. Equivalent levels of protection must be offered. In addition, the consumer must have the right to pursue any dispute with in his/her own country of residence. Prior to the conclusion of the contract, the process of finalising the contract should be clearly explained to the consumer. However, although access to the internet is growing all the time among individual consumers, they have been slower than businesses to explore the possibilities of buying products over the internet. Even in the United States, only 29% of the 53.5 million adults with internet access have made an online purchaseIn the United Kingdom, shopping ranks well below issues like education, business and e-mail access as reasons both for going online in the first place and for continuing to use the internet. The slow take-up of online shopping can be put down, at least in part, to a lack of confidence in buying through this new medium, and to fears about security and fraud.

When consumers commit themselves to a purchase online, they may not know the full identity of the retailer they are dealing with. They may not be told the terms and and conditions of the contract, or what their rights are when returning goods or obtaining redress. Nor may they have sufficient access to the retailer if something goes wrong – and the chance of something going wrong, such as non-delivery or damaged goods, is fairly high.

If electronic commerce is here to stay, national authorities, consumer organisations and businesses all have an interest in building consumer confidence by ensuring that consumers have the necessary access, protection, and service standards when buying. So much work is going on around the world on amending existing legislation and codes of practice, and on establishing new guidelines governing electronic commerce, that it would not be feasible to list all these initiatives here. The ones set out below are those which are most relevant to the consumer protection agenda.

The World Trade Organisation (WTO) has established a work programme on electronic commerce (adopted by the General Council on 25 September 1998), and published a study (Electronic *Commerce and the role of the WTO, WTO* Publications, March 1998), which identifies a range of issues that need to betackled, including access to the internet, regulation of content, security and privacy questions, and the legal and regulatory framework.

The Organisation for Economic Co-operation and Development (OECD) Committee on Consumer Policy is drafting guidelines (Guidelines for Consumer Protection in the Context *of Electronic Commerc*e), with detailed input from consumer representatives. The Transatlantic Consumer Dialogue (TACD) formulated recommendations on electronic commerce at a conference on 23-24 April 1999 in Brussels. These recommendations cover the establishment of minimum standards for consumer protection, urge the development of an International Convention on Privacy Protection, special protection for children, minimum standards for disclosure of information by suppliers, intellectual property rights, and call for discussion of a proposal to create a permanent global institution for consumer protection.

The European Union's *Proposal for European Parliament* and Council Directive on certain legal aspects of electronic commerce in the internal market, *DGXIV, COM(98) 586 Draft,* seeks to clarify five issues where uncertainty arises due to divergent national legislation:

1. place of establishment of service providers
2. commercial communications (advertising, direct marketing etc)
3. definition and transparency requirements
4. on-line conclusion of contracts
5. liability of intermediaries

6. implementation
7. strengthening enforcement mechanisms, facilitating the setting up of cross-border alternative dispute resolution systems, and a requirement for fast efficient legal redress in the on-line environment.
8. The European Union's Distance Selling Directive, which is still in the process of being transposed into national legislation across the EU, is also highly relevant.

Consumer organisations in a few European countries, including the Consumers' Association in the UK and Consumenten bondin the Netherlands, have recently launched a certification scheme which is run outside of the industry. Each participating consumer organisation provided information about what steps it and its government had taken on behalf of e-shoppers, and about the protection (if any) available for consumers making payment over the internet or wishing to return unsatisfactory goods.

Guidelines for e-commerce

Developed nations have been taken specific initiatives to develop guidelines for electronic commerce. In addition to these specific guidelines, electronic transactions are of course governed, like any other transactions, by existing rules, for example on advertising, marketing, and unfair contract terms. However, agreement on which laws should apply in cross-border transactions has been the subject of debate. Countries within the European Union are currently in the process of transposing the Distance Selling Directive into national law. This will have an important effect on electronic commerce.

Australia

In *Consumer Protection in Electronic Commerce; Principles and Key Issues, April 1998*, the government National Advisory Council on Consumer Affairs set out 12 principles for electronic commerce:

1. Consumers using electronic commerce are entitled to at least the same levels of protection as is provided by the laws and practices that apply to existing forms of commerce.

2. Consumers should be able to establish the identity and location of businesses with which they deal.

3. Consumers should have readily available clear and comprehensive information before and after any purchase of goods and/or services.

4. Sellers must state contract terms in clear, simple language.

5. Sellers should ensure they receive confirmed meaningful consent from consumers for a purchase of goods and/or services.

6. Consumers are entitled to receive clear information about the types of payment which will be accepted by the merchant or the payment provider.

7. Consumers are entitled to have their complaints and inquiries dealt with fairly and effectively.

8. Sellers should provide information to E-commerce guidelines and consumer rights: a country-by-country guide consumers about affordable and effective dispute resolution arrangements, when they are available.

9. Sellers must respect customer privacy.
10. Industry code administration bodies must closely monitor the application and effectiveness of their codes and be able to correct any deficiencies which are identified.
11. Each code-operating body should strive to maintain and promote consumer confidence in the global marketplace.
12. Governments should actively develop their consumer protection responsibilities. The Australian Consumers' Association magazine *Choice* has published a number of articles giving advice to consumers on electronic commerce.

Belgium

There are no specific guidelines for electronic commerce. The Belgian consumer organisation, Verbruikersunie, published guidance on electronic commerce in Budget & Droits No 138, April 1998.

Germany

There are no national guidelines for electronic commerce business practices yet. However, a 1997 law (Informations-und Kommunikationsdienste-Gesetz-IuKDG) covers electronic information and communication services, and contains consumer protection provisions in areas such as:

— identity of supplier

— data protection

— digital signatures and certification processes

— protection of children

— copyright.

The German consumer organisation, AgV, has published a number of studies and brochures giving advice to consumers on electronic commerce.

Japan

Effective approaches to consumer protection in electronic commerce (interim discussion of issues), Consumer Business Research Committee, Ministry of International Trade and *Industry, February 1998,* promotes the use of guidelines prepared by the Electronic commerce Promotion Council of Japan. These cover:

— consumer protection

— privacy and payment

— clarification of the law governing sales

— made in the home

— the need for strict enforcement of existing laws

— the need for greater education of consumers.

Sweden

The *Nordic Consumer Ombudsman's position paper* on trading and marketing on the Internet and in similar communication systems December 1998.

— marketing material

— clear provision of information

Throughout this survey Hong Kong is reffered rather than China, because the Hong Kong Consumer Council was one of the participating organisations, and because Hong Kong's consumer market remains distinct from that of the mainland.

— conclusion of contracts

— binding communications

— payment

— performance and complaints procedures

— use of e-mail

— processing of data

— marketing directed at children and young people.

United Kingdom

Various consultative documents have been issued by the Department of Trade and Industry. *Net benefit: the electronic commerce agenda for the UK* establishes some consumer and data protection principles, generally confirming that existing UK legislation covers internet transactions. The Office of Fair Trading issues extensive guidance to consumers on how to use the internet for shopping safely.

United States

The most important agency with regard to consumer protection and electronic commerce is the Federal Trade Commission (FTC). The FTC's philosophy is that the laws, regulations and guidelines it governs are as applicable to online transactions as other transactions. Various documents such as *Advertising and Marketing* on the internet: The Rules of the Road and *Guide to Online Payments* illustrate this position. In addition, the FTC has held hearings to help it understand how traditional consumer protections can best be translated into the new medium.

The one instance in which the FTC is moving in a new direction because of the internet is the privacy of children. In 1998 the United States Congress passed the Children's Online Privacy Protection Act. One essential element of online shopping is the passing of credit card details to the retailer over the internet, and the associated worries about these details reaching unauthorised third parties.

Although there are few rules specifically about credit cards and the internet, existing legislation is relevant in some countries. If the transaction involves a card and a Personal Identification Number, the Electronic Funds Transfer (EFT) Code says the consumer is liable for the first A$50 of any unauthorised transaction, unless the misuse stems from the consumer's negligence, in which case the consumer is liable for the total amount. If the transaction involved a card and no PIN, but does require a signature, the consumer is notable for any unauthorised transactions. Transactions involving a card and no PIN, not requiring a signature, are a grey area.

E-Transactions

Transactions are not limited to purchases of goods and services, but move along a spectrum beginning with information gathering and exchange, progressing to negotiation and decision to purchase, finally to completion of transaction and after sales support. In fact, at present, much of electronic commerce activity is concentrated in information gathering and exchange used to support purchase decisions.

As electronic commerce grows, the importance of sales transacted on-line is expected to increase. Business-to-business applications are driving the growth of electronic commerce, accounting for about 80 percent of Internet-based electronic commerce. Businesses have used EDI for over 25 years to conduct transactions with suppliers.

Now, lower costs and greater accessibility are causing businesses to move to the Internet, or to create hybrid networks through the use of intranets and extranets. In addition, an entirely new group of business users is coming on-line, mainly small and medium-sized firms that lack the resources required to support EDI. Consumer use of the Internet is still in its infancy. A Commerce Net/Nielsen survey conducted in 1997 found that only about 16 percent of Internet users in Canada and the United States have made purchases over the Internet.

As companies anticipate rapid growth in electronic commerce, significant investments are being made in the hardware, software and services required to support it. Global Internet-related investments were estimated to sum to about US$40 billion between 1995 and 1997, a portion of which was dedicated to electronic commerce. This US$40 billion in fact exceeded electronic commerce rev-enues.

An entirely new cadre of network-based intermediaries is developing, providing information search and evaluation, marketing, product and customer information, and secure on-line payment. Traditional sectors of advertising and delivery also play critical intermediary roles.

The United States is estimated to account for about 80 percent of worldwide Internet commerce revenue, followed by Canada at 5 percent. The United States accounts for between 70 and 85 percent of the top 100 sites by category of Internet purchases.

E-transactions: A Canadian Model

Canada has the second highest number of top-100 sites. Many people are predicting that electronic commerce will become a pervasive form of business within the next ten years. Assessing how likely this is to happen requires an examination of the intrinsic advantages and challenges of electronic commerce in general, and of specific types of transactions.

E-commerce encompasses three distinct types of transactions: those between businesses, those between businesses and consumers, and government services. These transactions are supported by the information technology infrastructure, consisting of hardware, software and enabling services. E-commerce provides a powerful means of diffusing the advantages of networking throughout the economy, based on a platform provided by the information technology sector. This sector is strong and growing, as demonstrated by increasing shares of gross domestic product (GDP).

In the United States, the information technology sector has grown from just under 5 percent of the economy in 1985 to just under 8 percent in 1997. Given that prices for information technology goods and services have fallen dramatically – for example, the cost of microprocessing computing power has fallen from US$230 to US$3.42 per MIPS (millions of instructions per second) since 1991 – this increasing share of GDP is even more impressive.

The story is the same in Canada. The information and communications technology sector accounted for 5 percent of GDP in 1990, increasing to over 7 percent in 1996. This sector accounted for 30 percent of total economic growth between 1990 and 1996, with compound annual growth rates of 7.6 percent during this period, compared with 1.5 percent for the total economy. Electronic commerce will spur continuing growth in the information technology sector.

Given its potential to change how business is done, electronic commerce will have even broader impacts, promising to accelerate growth not only in the information technology sector itself, but also across all sectors of the economy, such as manufacturing and retailing. The intrinsic advantage of the Internet as a platform for electronic commerce rests on the open, non-proprietary nature of the network: the Internet allows businesses to use a global, interactive means of infrmation exchange at a low cost. While some would argue that such a capability already exists through existing communications networks such as telephone, fax or proprietary networks, the Internet offers an unmatchable combination of interactivity, versatility, low cost and speed.

The implications of worldwide, low-cost information exchange are profound. The full potential of computerized design, manufacturing, delivery and services may now be realised by linking all parts of a distribution chain together, from product concept, design, testing, and manufacturing to marketing, after sales and service. For example, software designers and automotive manufacturers can test concepts and prototypes with users, and demand forecasts can be immediately passed from marketing to production and the supply chain.

As a result, efficiency and productivity are increased through lower procurement costs, reduced processing errors, reduced inventories, and faster time to market. For example, by linking marketing to manufacturing and procurement, IBM improved inventory turns and experienced savings of US$500 million due to lower investment and operating costs.

Automotive companies have reduced material flow to the supply chain from up to six to less than two weeks. Companies are also adopting the Internet as a base for business transactions to gain a competitive advantage, often at the insistence of other business partners in a supply chain. These forces are expected to result in the rapid growth of business-to-business electronic commerce. From the consumer's perspective, electronic commerce offers significant benefits.

Convenience, increased access to information, lower prices, and choice are benefits cited most often by consumers. For example, a small business, Unique Patterns Design of Halifax, Nova Scotia, is able to offer custom patterns that are tailor-made for each customer. Electronic commerce is also being used to support purchases made in conventional retail channels, as it allows consumers to gather information and comparison shop on-line. Products and services most suited to electronic sale are those that are information intensive and can be delivered digitally, or tangible products that do not require tactile examination and can be easily shipped.

Early leaders in consumer electronic commerce have fit this profile, most notably financial services, computer hardware and software, travel, entertainment, and books and CDs. Electronic commerce has widespread benefits beyond those related to the transaction of business. Governments at all levels are turning to the Internet as a means of increasing the range, reach and availability of their services. Services are available 24 hours a day, seven days a week, independent of location. The costs of providing these services can be significantly reduced for both users and governments.

Electronic delivery of government services will also facilitate the future integration of government services from different departments and different levels of government. Other public sector institutions such as those in the education and health sectors are also using the Internet as an affordable tool to increase the reach of their services.

Computer-based training can provide information which is immediately available and tailored to specific needs, making the goal of lifelong learning more attainable. In the health care sector, the Internet is being used to allow rural or remote doctors, clinics and hospitals to access specialized knowledge and services usually found only in urban centers, and to diffuse information to the public.

Most broadly, networking promises to allow citizens to participate more fully in society and create new sense of community through greatly improved means of communications.

The potential for electronic commerce is real. However, limiting factors exist, many based on the Internet itself, including issues of universal access, governance, and the future capacity of the underlying network.Access to the Internet, while growing, is far from universal: in Canada, 36 percent of households own a personal computer, and 13 percent had Internet connections in 1997. If Internet access from home, work, school and elsewhere is included, access is just over 30 percent. The majority of large businesses and an estimated 43 percent of small businesses have Internet access. While these levels of access are among the best in the world, they do not come close to the near-universal penetration of established communications technologies such as the telephone.

E-commerce promises to transform the conduct of business, consumer and government transactions, offering the benefits of more efficient supply chains, greater convenience and choice, and lower cost of doing business. However, before these benefits are realised, businesses and consumers want to know that transactions are private and secure, that legal and financial frameworks exist to support transactions and that the information infrastructure works.

Many possible scenarios exist for the future of electronic commerce. Optimists assume that these issues will be addressed and that electronic commerce will continue to grow. The contrary, pessimistic belief is that growth in electronic commerce, particularly growth in on-line sales, will stagnate as underlying problems remain unresolved, which could lead to a spin-drying of the Internet into smaller managed proprietary networks. Electronic commerce promises to be a major generator of jobs and growth in the next century, through improvements in the productivity of business, growth in consumer transactions, and development of the supporting information technology infrastructure.

Experience has shown that early leaders quickly establish market dominance. Those who enter first are able to help shape evolving rules as well as business and consumer behaviour. Canada enjoys many advantages that position it to compete effectively in electronic commerce.

Canada has the highest standing of post-secondary education enrolment in the world, ranked first in knowledge workers by the World Economic Forum. Its telecommunications infrastructure is world class – it has among the lowest telephone costs in the world and the lowest Internet access charges among G-7 countries; it is second only to the United States in telephone mainlines and Internet hosts per capita among G-7 countries; and it has many pioneering telecommunications and information technology companies that are recognized worldwide.

Analysis of the challenges facing the use and growth of electronic commerce, reflecting views from business, consumers, provinces and territories, as well as international organizations, points to four key areas for electronic commerce action in Canada. Most business relationships, whether between a consumer and a company or between firms, require a strong element of confidence and trust. The impersonal and remote nature of electronic commerce places a heavy burden on the need for means to reduce or eliminate risk.

Security, privacy and consumer protection are all required to instill trust in electronic commerce, for both businesses and consumers. A body of rules that govern how business and government transactions are conducted has developed over time. To remove barriers to the use of electronic commerce, these rules need to be examined to assess how they apply to the digital world, and adapted where necessary, to create a level playing field which is predictable and consistent for all kinds of commerce. Electronic commerce will not grow without a strong platform that includes network access and availability, and open standards.Electronic commerce is part of a broader process of economic, social and cultural change, characterized by the globalization of markets and the shift toward an economy based on knowledge and information.

Opportunities for jobs and growth created by electronic commerce need to be distributed as widely as possible among citizens, consumers and businesses, through development of skills and awareness, and government leadership as model users. The Canadian electronic commerce strategy is based on the recognition that the private sector has the key role in developing and expanding electronic commerce in Canada. Government's role is to provide a supportive and responsive policy environment for businesses and consumers, one that allows for market flexibility while ensuring a minimum baseline for a fair marketplace.

Countries that can provide such environments will be better positioned to compete internationally. To this end, the Canadian government and private sector are working together to implement the Canadian electronic commerce strategy. Electronic commerce is intrinsically global. The actions of any one country will have limited impact unless they are part of a larger international framework.

Canada is not developing domestic policies in isolation, but is committed to working with other countries to develop the international frameworks necessary to make electronic commerce grow.

Organisation for Economic Co-operation and Development: Canada's commitment to the international agenda is demonstrated by hosting the OECD Ministerial Conference on Electronic Commerce, in Ottawa, October 7-9, 1998. The conference includes governments and international organizations as well as business, labour and consumer interests. It leads to the establishment of agreements and action plans spelling out the current and future roles of government, international organizations and the private sector in addressing key electronic commerce issues. The Ministerial Conference represents the culmination of a series of electronic commerce conferences held by the OECD, beginning with a conference focussing on consumer views held in Paris in March 1997, followed by a conference focussing on business views held in Turku, Finland, in November 1997.

Asia Pacific Economic Cooperation: In November 1997, APEC leaders agreed to the development of a work plan for electronic commerce. Under the direction of a task force co-chaired by Australia and Singapore, the first phase of the work plan – consisting of benchmarking electronic commerce developments in member countries – has been completed. The second phase of the program is being reviewed by leaders at their meeting in Kuala Lumpur in November 1998, including the development of an electronic commerce vision statement to promote the use of electronic commerce in the region, and the development of recommendations for technical cooperation and capacity building, public sector use of electronic commerce, and outreach programs targeted at small and medium-sized enterprises (SMEs).In addition to the Task Force, APEC Ministers of Telecommunications and Information Industries approved a reference framework for action to guide the work of telecommunications groups on a range of electronic commerce issues.

World Trade Organization: Canada has also taken a leadership role in ensuring that the trade disciplines of the WTO apply to electronic commerce. At the second WTO Ministerial in May 1998, members agreed to launch a comprehensive study of the trade policy aspects of electronic commerce, with a view to providing recommendations to ministers for future actions by the third Ministerial in 1999.

Free Trade Agreement of the Americas (FTAA): The FTAA has formed the Joint Government-Private Sector Committee of Experts on Electronic Commerce to make recommendations to ministers on how to increase and broaden the benefits of electronic commerce and, in particular, how electronic commerce should be dealt with in the context of FTAA negotiations. The committee is developing working guidelines and will be delivering recommendations for ministers prior to their October 1999 meeting.

G-8 Pilot Project: "A Global Market for SMEs": The project, being coordinated by Japan, the United States and the European Commission, involves 20 countries and international organizations, including Canada. Its overall objective is to provide a framework and implementation plan for global coordination and cooperation in electronic commerce, focussing on SMEs. Business and consumer transactions require assurances of trust – trust that transactions are secure and private, that transactions are supported by complete and accurate information, and that consumer redress is available.

Measures developed for conventional commerce may be inadequate to provide trust in the digital economy. For example, while once data were held securely within an organization, either in paper-based files or in internal computer systems, now the Internet and hybrid forms such as extranets and intranets allow for potentially widespread information access. Issues of security once related only to law enforcement, not to protecting on-line transactions. Government baselines exist for business and consumer protection, but key issues – such as the verification of the identity of parties and the determination of transaction jurisdictions within a global context – remain unaddressed. In addressing these issues, both governments and the private sector have a role. Governments can legislate or regulate, while looking to the private sector to introduce voluntary codes and develop technological solutions.

Many of the elements of building trust involve both federal, provincial and territorial governments – the Uniform Law Conference of Canada, and the Consumer Measures Committee established under the Internal Trade Agreement, are pivotal in establishing model laws and providing guidance on consistent national approaches. Secure electronic transactions can be provided through the use of cryptographic technologies and certification authorities. These authorities, by binding parties to their respective digital signatures, provide authentication as to the identity of the transacting parties. Cryptographic technologies also provide for the integrity and confidentiality of the messages that are exchanged, and ensure that neither party to the transaction can deny its participation in the exchange of information (otherwise known as non-repudiation).

The benefits of cryptography for electronic commerce, privacy protection and crime prevention are clear. It is equally true that cryptographic technologies can be used to hide criminal activity and to threaten national security. Investigations, prosecutions, and the enforcement of laws and regulations could be hampered without lawful access to the evidence of illegal activity.

Canada does not restrict the freedom of choice of individuals or businesses to import or use cryptography. Users are free to determine what kinds of authentication and encryption products and services they need. Canada controls the export of cryptography along with 32 other nations that are members of the Wassenaar Arrangement, which stipulates which products require export permits and which do not. Canadian cryptography policy is under review in order to ensure that it contributes to the realisation of Canada's goal to be a leader in the use of electronic commerce, and to ensure that it reflects an appropriate balance among business, human rights and privacy interests, public safety and law enforcement, and national security interests.

The policy, released in the fall of 1998, provides greater certainty for the business community, more confidence for consumers and support for law enforcement and national security. The strategy for the protection of privacy is to put the Canadian Standards Association National Standard into effect through light legislation, complemented by private sector action and consumer awareness.The Government of Canada's fall 1998 private sector information privacy legislation strikes a balance between industry's interest in compiling and using personal information and the consumer's right to have personal information adequately protected. Consultations held during early 1998 found that there is strong support for using the Canadian Standards Association (CSA) Model Code for the Protection of Personal Information (also referred to as the CSA National Standard), as the basis for any such law, and the Office of the Privacy Commissioner of Canada as the oversight agency.

There is also general agreement on the need for a consistent approach among federal and provincial privacy laws for the private sector. While to date, only Quebec has legislation, there is strong support for the use of the CSA Standard as the starting point for any new legislation. Canada has led the world in developing a National Standard for the protection of privacy. This Standard, developed by businesses, consumers and governments, addresses the way organizations collect, use, disclose and protect information, and the way individuals access personal information. An informed public is vital to the protection of personal information. Both the private sector and governments can work to raise awareness of privacy issues and ensure that citizens know their rights and the best way to protect their personal data. A good example is the partnership of the federal government and Stentor to fund a multimedia game, Privacy Playground: The First Adventure of the Three Little Cyberpigs, to raise privacy awareness among children. The government encourages the development and use of such technologies for the lawful protection of its citizens. The Working Group on Consumers and Electronic Commerce, composed of consumer and business associations and governments, is finalizing Canadian guidelines on consumer protection in electronic commerce. The guidelines define consumer protection requirements and provide the basis for development of voluntary and legislative measures related to consumer information, contract formation, privacy, security and redress.

A range of consumer protection legislation already exists in Canada, in both provincial and federal spheres. The Consumer Measures Committee established under the Agreement on Internal Trade is considering ways to address consumer protection in electronic commerce. Consumer Protection Rights in Canada in the Context of Electronic Commerce, a report prepared by the legal firm of Gowling, Strathy & Henderson, is being used as a basis for discussion.

The Government of Canada is also looking at provisions under the Competition Act governing deceptive trade practices and misleading advertising. Governments, business and consumer groups agree that voluntary codes can play a vital role in areas not covered by legislation. For example, the Canadian Code of Practice for Consumer Debit Card Services, established in 1992 by consumer groups, businesses, and provincial and federal governments, has successfully guided consumer protection practices of financial institutions.

The Working Group on Consumers and Electronic Commerce will be addressing consumer awareness in the guidelines on consumer protection in electronic commerce, including the need for consumers to be provided with advice on how to minimize the risks entailed in electronic transactions, and legal rights and obligations. Technology can provide the tools to make information available to consumers. Examples include posting information on laws that apply in different jurisdictions, and posting seals of approval on Web sites that meet defined criteria.

As new forms of business practice evolve, marketplace rules play a critical role in creating codes of conduct – for example in the use of electronic signatures, the assignment of liability, and the protection of trademarks. Without clear rules, the use and growth of electronic commerce will be stalled. The overriding need is to remove barriers to the use of electronic commerce by clarifying how these rules apply to the digital economy and updating them where necessary. The objective is to ensure that equivalent treatment is provided for digital and non-digital transactions in a consistent and predictable manner.

Business has clearly stated that clarifying marketplace rules should be the government's top priority. Consistency among and between provinces and territories and the federal government is critical, particularly for legal and commercial frameworks. The Uniform Law Conference of Canada (ULCC) is playing a leadership role in this regard. All government and business operations are subject to law. Law has traditionally presumed the presence of paper records – that presumption is no longer valid. As a result, the application of law to paperless transactions may lead to uncertain results. Governments are acting to make adjustments to laws to bring certainty to the use of technology.

Over 300 federal statutes contain provisions requiring documents to be "in writing" or equivalent words. Rather than have each department amend legislation piecemeal, the Government of Canada's fall 1998 electronic documents legislation allows departments to adopt a set of general provisions authorizing the use of electronic communications. Provinces and territories are being encouraged to undertake statutory reforms along similar lines, as set out in the Uniform Electronic Commerce Actapproved in principle by the ULCC in August 1998. Many legal rules and the law of evidence assume the existence of paper, signed or original records. While most electronic records are, in practice, being admitted in litigation, the courts have struggled with the traditional rules of evidence with inconsistent results. The ULCC approved the Uniform Electronic Evidence Actin August 1998, which evaluates the integrity of an electronic record by considering evidence of the reliability of the record-keeping system that generated the record.

The federal Department of Justice has proposed amending the Canada Evidence Act, to make it consistent with the ULCC Uniform Electronic Evidence Act. Provinces and territories will also consider amending their legislation to reflect the ULCC Uniform Evidence Act. The challenge is to link the electronic signature to the person signing the electronic document. The Government of Canada is proposing that what makes an electronic signature trustworthy is the use of a reliable technology, such as digital signature technology, combined with a reliable certification authority (CA), such as those operating under the Government of Canada Public Key Infrastructure (GOC PKI) and those CAs that have cross-certification or are otherwise recognized by the GOC PKI.Internet Service Providers and other Internet intermediaries have expressed concern about the possible extent of their liability with respect to areas covered by a number of federal and provincial laws – e.g. obscenity, copyright, consumer protection, fraud and defamation – which may result from actions of their clients.

The uncertainty surrounding liability may be an impediment to investment in electronic commerce and to its pace of development. The OECD has reviewed legal frameworks applicable to content in its member countries. The Government of Canada has released for comment a study on Internet content-related liability and is currently analyzing the issue. In the longer term, impacts on other aspects of legal frameworks such as corporate and competition laws will be of interest.The view of both Canadian and international taxation authorities has been that current tax systems and structures founded on basic principles of neutrality, fairness, certainty and simplicity will continue to be appropriate to address the changes brought about by electronic transactions.

Attention has been focussed on ensuring that tax administration can keep up with changes in the market. The Minister of National Revenue's Advisory Committee on Electronic Commerce issued a report in April 1998 titled Electronic Commerce and Canada's Tax Administrationthat examines how existing taxation systems apply to electronic commerce. The report examines, among other issues, jurisdictional questions (e.g. the concept of a permanent residency), impacts of disintermediation (the splintering of intermediary services) on tax collection, and tax compliance. The Government of Canada's response to the report was released in the fall of 1998.

Given the global reach of electronic commerce, most of these issues can only be dealt with in an international context. Canada is participating with other OECD member countries in developing international implementation strategies that will include the implications of electronic commerce on tax treaties, transfer pricing guidelines, the application of consumption taxes and customs duties and tariffs. In May 1998, WTO members agreed to refrain from applying customs duties on the electronic products and services delivered electronically and to review this decision at the third WTO Ministerial meeting in 1999.

A two-track approach, linking a comprehensive WTO work program on electronic commerce with a moratorium on customs duties, was based on a proposal submitted by Canada to the General Council in April 1998, and was later adopted by ministers of the QUAD (Canada, the U.S., the Commission of the European Union and Japan). Financial firms are rapidly expanding their delivery channels, by using new communications technologies to broaden the geographic scope of their operations and obtain more convenient, cost-effective links with customers. Financial intermediaries, such as banks, credit unions, brokerages and insurance agencies, are supplementing personal branch banking with on-line services through the Internet, telephone networks and automated teller machines.

Intermediaries are applying new digital technologies to reduce their cash-handling costs and simplify payment processing. With the help of new technology, specialized financial service providers are entering the sector, increasing competition and leading to the unbundling of services in certain markets. For example, brokers offering both trading and securities market information are now competing with on-line brokers who simply trade and provide no other services. Changing delivery channels are intrinsically linked to opportunities to create new products and services. Technologies such as risk management tools, digital certification and cryptography create potential for new products such as automated sourcing of capital, on-line clearing and payment intermediaries, and information brokerage. Canada's financial institutions are involved in the development of new technology that may improve the efficiency of transactions and consumer convenience while helping to ensure privacy and the security of financial information.

These changes are having an impact on the nature and structure of the Canadian financial services sector. The (MacKay) Task Force on the Future of the Canadian Financial Services Sector, which reported to the government in September 1998, made recommendations aimed at ensuring the sector's ability to meet global competitive challenges and the interests of consumers, and to take advantage of technological advances.

The global nature of electronic commerce also raises issues related to cross-border transactions in financial services. These issues are being examined by both national governments and international bodies such as the Basle Committee on Banking Supervision and the World Trade Organization. Intellectual property (IP) laws establish the rules for the ownership and use of key types of digital content central to the development of electronic commerce, such as music, computer programs, video and multimedia works.

In addition to the need for clear rules on ownership and access to content, other key IP issues include liability of Internet intermediaries, trademarks and domain names, and database protection. New international agreements and other forms of cooperation are being considered to address these concerns, through the WIPO, the FTAA, APEC and the OECD. Canada is an active player in these discussions. Canada's national IP legislation is being reviewed to determine whether it needs to be adapted and whether it will be in Canada's interest to undertake any new international obligations.

WIPO member countries adopted two new treaties in December 1996, the WIPO Copyright Treaty and the WIPO Performances and Phonograms Treaty. These treaties give right-holders including authors, performers and record producers an exclusive right to make their works, performances and sound recordings available through interactive media on a demand basis.

Canadian banks are partnering in the development of new electronic payment systems based on smart cards that allow consumers to purchase goods and services using prepaid electronic "value" in lieu of cash. The value is typically stored on an integrated circuit in a plastic card and can be read using special devices including point of sale terminals. Special encryption software helps ensure the security of the electronic value. Some electronic money systems allow for the transfer of value over communications networks as well as direct, person-to-person transfers. They also contain provisions with respect to copy protection and rights management information, among other new rights.

Canada signed the WIPO treaties in December 1997, but has not yet ratified them. In July 1998, the government released two discussion papers that consider what, if any, amendments to the Canadian Copyright Actwould be necessary in order to comply with the treaties. Canada's copyright legislation, as amended in 1997, already provides a framework for copyright protection that is largely up-to-date compared with legislation in many countries.

The Canadian government is currently analyzing the issue of the liability of Internet intermediaries, such as Internet Service Providers, for intellectual property infringements, as part of its ongoing consultations on Internet content-related liability. WIPO is also considering certain aspects of liability, including applicable law and jurisdiction.

Ongoing reform of the Canadian and international domain name systems (DNS) has highlighted the need to ensure that these systems and other Internet practices reflect IP rights and obligations appropriately, notably trade-marks. One major structural problem is that the Internet is international, whereas trade-marks law is national in scope. WIPO, with private sector input, has convened an international process to solicit recommendations on IP issues associated with the DNS. Progress on the reform of the Canadian DNS has also led to the recognition that a balanced approach is needed.In the context of increased availability of data through electronic means, databases are more and more important in a knowledge-based economy.

Industry Canada and Canadian Heritage are engaging in a consultative process with major stakeholders to assess how Canadian laws apply to protection of databases, and whether a special form of IP protection should be developed for databases.

Electronic financial services

The banking and finance sector was one of the first industry sectors to benefit from the use of information technology more generally. Early computers were used for scientific and military purposes, not for commerce.

The banking and finance sector has been a rapid adopter of e-commerce. The sector displays many characteristics that will facilitate the adoption and extension of e-commerce activities, such as the importance of product over location, many of its key services are easily virtualised, and great importance is placed on quick response times. For some time now most of the transactions between banks in the payments system have been undertaken electronically. Banking systems have also progressively automated deposit taking and payments. Key developments have included the now widespread acceptance and utilisation of ATMs and EFTPOS.

Use of Internet banking is also growing rapidly. Of the 1.7 million Australians using the Internet regularly, nearly 150 000 are involved in Internet banking. This is a threefold increase from a year ago. Internet consultancy www.consult projects that there will be about 270 000 Internet banking users by the beginning of 2 000. Most users are expected to extend their existing banking relationships. While the four big domestic banks have Internet-banking offerings, the Commonwealth Bank is the largest.

Forty five per cent of regular Internet banking users bank online with the Commonwealth Bank and nearly 30 per cent with Westpac. National Australia Bank is Australia's biggest banker to small business. Users of NAB Internet Banking, are reported to have increased from 8 000 to 26 000 in two months and are signing up at twice the rate of personal customers. The key attributes that the commercial banks offer in their Internet banking facilities typically include:

1. review transaction details;

2. transfer funds between accounts;
3. pay bills;
4. transaction records and account statements;
5. buying or selling of funds that can be used in other e-commerce sites;
6. communicate securely with the bank;
7. standard fees, or sometimes, lower banking fees per transaction; and
8. customer convenience in terms of 24 hours a day, seven days a week service, without queues and from the comfort of one's home or office.

E-banks

E-banks are able to design their business without wasteful and lower value 'bricks and mortar' assets and liabilities. They may have a 'second mover advantage' because they do not have to face the cost of restructuring. There is evidence that they are able to offer financial services at prices well below traditional firms. This has not had an impact in the Australian banking industry at present. This may be because the traditional banks still offered a wider range of services that customers considered safe or perhaps reflect the fact that Australia's major banks have been quick to develop their own relatively sophisticated online banking functionality. The Commonwealth Bank was online in December 1995 and had Internet Banking in February 1997. Nevertheless, traditional banking approaches are increasingly under competitive pressure. Relationship marketing is becoming more difficult as more organisations enter the market.

Banking and finance institutions now face competition from online trading organisations that gain a complete picture of a consumer's financial relationships by building around the equity holdings and into banking, insurance, superannuation, etc. This can lead to an unbundling and rebundling of services. Bill-paying over the Internet is likely to become usiness-as-usual within just a few years. The Gartner Group predicts that in two years virtually all banks will offer online bill payment, and industry analysts believe that Internet portals such as America Online (AOL) and Yahoo! will soon be offering online payment under their own brands. AOL's Rob Shenk says, 'A lot of people have stock portfolios, but everyone has a checking account. So it's a much more elemental service.'A reluctance on the part of customers to switch to new providers may make sense: good financial relationships should not be thrown away for the sake of small short– term savings.

Growth of Internet banking and new competitors does not imply the end of traditional banks or financial services brokers. Reflecting existing strengths and consumer awareness, it may be a matter of changes in roles and involvement at different levels. One example of the transfer of value from the industry is the bundling of financial services as part of another transaction, e.g. buying a car, or factory equipment. The finance can be provided or facilitated by a party other than one from the industry, distancing banking and finance from their customers, or replacing them.

However, if banking and finance take a higher view of their role, using a business event model this opens opportunities for creating value and improving relationships using e-commerce in ways which it would be too expensive to do face-to-face.

There are issues here of who has the 'right' or credibility to provide the service, i.e. who bundles whom. The transfer of value occurs if the service that brokers offer is unbundled. Brokers currently offer advice, risk management and execution. Risk management could be unbundled to the insurance sector, or new participants could enter using e-commerce services.

Banks from smaller countries in Scandinavia and Europe have been very aggressive in penetrating larger European markets with an Internet banking presence. Is there a scope for entry of banks from abroad into Australia using a similar strategy? There is no evidence to indicate that there has been a significant transfer of value to overseas firms through widespread offshore banking or other financial transactions. In contrast, there is anecdotal evidence to indicate that despite falling transaction costs and improved information, many investors find overseas investment or deposit in overseas banks to be too risky. Industry sources indicate however that there is some scope for migration of this service, albeit over time.

The inflow of value from overseas is not significant and would be predominantly from the acquisition of international banking operations by the Australian banks and any associated movement of functions to Australia. For example The Bank of New Zealand owned by NAB operates its Internet site and undertakes all its processing in Australia including monitoring and supporting its ATM network. E-commerce is a major enabler of this, specifically EDI, the Internet and other dedicated networking systems. The opportunities opened up by e-commerce is a factor driving change in the banking and financial services sector.

Use of e-commerce is shifting demand and supply in the sector to lower cost more convenient service delivery channels. In meeting the broad range of financial service needs that customers have within a single entity, the distinction between banks and other traditional financial service roles is becoming blurred.

The potential of online financial services has reduced many barriers to entry and is increasing competitive pressures. It is likely that cost savings that will result from this process will be passed on to consumers.

When looking at quantitative analysis of the sector it seems reasonable to factor in a wide range of direct changes:

1. direct labour savings extending the staff reductions the sector is already achieving;
2. banking is also expected to be able to disintermediate other input costs, particularly those that relate to the operation of branch networks. To reflect this it can be assumed that a small reduction in inputs of construction and paper products is achieved;
3. reflecting the increased convenience of online banking and financial services, time savings should be included as an efficiency gain for other industries that use the services of the sector as well as households;
4. the sector has already boosted expenditure to purchase e-commerce inputs and these are already factored in to the base case forecasts.
5. for the moment it is assumed that this sector will not face greater international competition or experience a significant boost in exports from e-commerce.

The IT industries have a number of unusual characteristics. They are among the fastest growing industries. Technological change is rapid and product life cycles are short. Most product and service prices are falling rather than rising. Convergence in the industries is leading to the increasing inter-relation and interdependence of computing, communications and the media. This is also profoundly changing the structure and dynamics of the IT industries.

Change in the IT industries and their capacity is driving change in the use of e-commerce while the IT industries are also being driven by changes in e-commerce usage. The IT industries extend through a value chain including electronics to computing and telecomm-unications platforms, office equipment and consumer electronics, telecommunications carriage and services, IT services and to information and entertainment services. Computing power has been doubling every 18 months for the past 30 years. At the same time, the average price of a transistor has fallen by six orders of magnitude, due to microprocessor development.

In just six years, the cost of microprocessor computing power decreased from $230 to $3.42 per MIPS. No other manufactured item has decreased in cost so far, so fast. Whether traded or non-traded, the IT industries are growing strongly at a rate in excess of ten per cent per annum.

It is estimated that approximately 500 000 Australians are employed by, or spend a substantial part of their time engaged in the commercial activities of the information industries. Official statistics indicate that use of IT in Australia by the private sector is high: companies employing 100 or more people are almost fully computerised; 50 per cent of smaller companies are computerised and this rate is growing.Use of e-commerce by the IT industries.

The IT industries have been rapid adopters of e-commerce technologies and business models. The biggest advances in this sector have been in business-to-business e-commerce. More use is being made of e-commerce to facilitate the purchase of goods and services by consumers, but it is still very much behind the magnitude of sales made between businesses. The greater use of e-commerce in the sector has the potential to add value or reduce costs in the following areas:

1. value chain disintermediation;
2. enhancing value in sales and after sales support activities; and
3. improved operations.

The IT industry is now able to deliver many of its products using e-commerce. Items such as software and documentation that traditionally had to be shipped can now be delivered online. Hardware is also becoming upgradeable without the need to physically replace parts. Software can be delivered online to allow customers to upgrade hardware such as modem cards.

In general, there are many areas where businesses in the IT industries or their customers are using e-commerce to reduce supply chain costs, or enhance their convenience. Warehousing, inventory and the volume of product in the cycle are much less than would otherwise be. This has also reduced the real estate required to store the inventory.

The number of suppliers has been reduced, Cisco now tends to deal with the original manufacturer and manufacturers of components. The additional suppliers added time to the process and also forced Cisco to be a manufacturer. In some cases, Cisco has eliminated its own involvement. The other major elimination that has occurred is in the number of trips provided by the transport sector, now that many deliveries take place directly from the supplier to the customer. Cisco builds virtually all its products to order, so there are very few off-the-shelf products. Before the company established an Internet sales capability, ordering a product could be complicated. Generally, an engineer at the customer site knew what type of product was needed and how it should be configured. The engineer communicated this information to his procurement department who then created the purchase order and sent it to Cisco via fax, phone or email.

A Cisco customer service administrator entered the order into Cisco's system. If the order went through 'clean', it would be booked and production scheduled within 24 hours. Nearly one out of four orders didn't get a 'clean' bill of health, however. Instead, when Cisco's system tried to validate the order, it discovered an error in how the product was configured. The 'dirty' order would be rejected, the customer contacted and the procurement cycle would begin again. In July 1996, Cisco rolled out its web-based ordering and configuring system. Today, that same engineer can sit down at a PC, configure the product online, know immediately if there are any errors and route the order to the procurement department. Because the customer's pricing structure is already programmed into the Cisco site, the authorised purchaser can complete the order with a few keystrokes.

Rather than calling Cisco to find out the status of the order, invoice or account information, a customer with the proper authorisation can access the information directly on the website. With the online pricing and configuration tools, about 98 per cent of the orders go through the system the first time, saving time both at Cisco and the customer's site. Lead times have dropped two to three days, and customers' productivity has increased an average of 20 per cent per order.

E-commerce is now fundamental to Cisco. Eighty per cent of orders in Australia are generated by e-commerce, up from 40 per cent three years ago. The objective is to grow the orders received electronically to 90 per cent next year. Cisco's business is $400 million in Australia and $12 billion worldwide. As well as the benefits to Cisco, this use of e-commerce impacts on a lot of businesses that buy from Cisco.

The use of online ordering has reduced the headcount in the order entry department by one in the last two years, although the volume of orders received has tripled. The quality of order entry has also improved, due to online checking at the time of entry, from a 30 per cent error rate to less than two per cent. Customers can also check delivery schedules online. The whole process is more profitable, and better for customers. Orders are faster, cleaner, are checked against the manufacturing cycle, while more orders can be processed using fewer people. Customer satisfaction has increased from 3.5 to four, with five being a perfect score. The users of the system, Cisco's customers, are medium to large businesses. Cisco does not sell direct to consumers.

Cisco is also working on supply chain management, aiming and succeeding in being a 'virtual organisation'. Suppliers provide components, such as chips and boards. Cisco demands that suppliers be online. This has eliminated complex processes, and made a tighter link to manufacturers with no middlemen. Effectively, 50 per cent of the physical boxes are delivered to the customer direct from Cisco's supplier.

Cisco has an Intranet used by employees and suppliers alike. Suppliers access the same forecasting information as Cisco. Eighty to 85 per cent of software is now downloaded by customers, whereas it was previously distributed by CD-ROM. It used to cost $125 to send a CD, downloads cost $5. This has also eliminated the deliveries of CDs. All product information, including technical information is available online. Eighty per cent of technical information is now sourced online by customers. Customers can also enrol for seminars online. This has achieved the objective of increasing customer satisfaction, while saving on the cost of distributing physical documentation. Internally, expense accounts are submitted online and profiled automatically. Payments are made by direct credit to the employee's bank account. This system is used by all 18 000 employees worldwide. Cisco hopes to have invoicing online soon. The main benefits to Cisco of e-commerce have been the reduced head count, reduced inventory, reduced paperwork, and reduced direct costs such as with the downloading of software. IT industries will also have to purchase more electronic inputs from new intermediaries in order to engage in greater e-commerce. The indications are that these costs will be relatively modest, certainly in proportion to the potential efficiency gains that IT industries are likely to obtain.

The use of e-commerce is also increasing the complexity of the information technology requirements. Many organisations are outsourcing the management of their information technology systems. There is a transfer of value into the IT sector brought in by the outsourcing of IT and services from other industries, such as government, finance and travel. Greater use of e-commerce is likely to drive changes in the way that business is done in the IT industries. It appears that there will be swings transferring value between activities in the IT industries. The first is the potential transfer from hardware to software—this is predominantly caused by the rapid reductions in costs of hardware while software has maintained its value.

E-commerce has not been a major driver of this. There is a transfer from commodity manufacture to mass customisation. This has also resulted in a transfer in value from whole items to components. This is being driven by the varied nature of e-commerce and the many applications for the use of information technology in this area, resulting in the need to customise hardware.For value creation there are very strong possibilities in many sectors, particularly in government. There are cost saving and productivity improvements possible from the use of e-commerce.

The opportunity to create value is also high in IT services. IBM believe that software and especially services will be the drivers for growth, while the value creation in hardware is lessening. This means a transfer of value within the IT sector from hardware to software and services. This transfer of value is leading to a move from commodity manufacture to mass customisation, particularly for large customers, and the management of the assembly. The trend to network computing is leading to the value being held in the network not on the hard drive of the computer.

One of the issues for all industries today, is how a business becomes an e-business. That is, not only setting firms up online, but helping them to deal with customers online, and integration into their existing systems and processes. IBM has used it own experience to assist its customers. The process of convergence is also reshaping what it is that businesses in the IT industries will offer in future. Some companies that have been established in the industry for some time have responded dramatically to challenges and opportunities raised by e-commerce. IBM is in the IT sector, but also heavily involved in the e-commerce sector.

The IT sector is a key facilitator for e-commerce, and will be one of the big winners. Some in Australia focus on creating the hardware sides of IT and e-commerce in Australian (chip and other hardware manufacture) but IBM does not see enough critical mass in Australia to support these hardware efforts. Rather, IBM believes that Australia's opportunities are in services and content development which have a much higher value add. The value proposition in the e-commerce world is different than for many other industries. In manufacturing, automotive for example, a basic model car is developed as the lowest common denominator, then features are added to add value.

In e-commerce, the 'lowest common denominator' is the high end or perfect product, from which features are removed to subtract value. The model is more akin to book publishing, where the hardcover is published, and some time later a cheaper paperback is released. Time is also a driver of value, for example the latest stock prices on websites are available at a higher cost than those whose publication is delayed.

The growth of e-commerce internationally has led to a huge demand for high quality IT personnel. Many international countries are willing to pay quality IT personnel more than Australian companies. This is particularly the case with start-up IT companies. The transfer of value to or from overseas can occur with the rise of the Internet and network computing, with the offering of remote services, for example, remote education, application development, etc. The direction of the service flow will determine the direction of the value transfer, i.e. whether Australia positions to provide remote education services, or is the recipient of them. Australia has some advantages over other countries that are resulting in an inflow of value from overseas.

1. Well educated and technically competent workforce;
2. Well positioned for Asian markets;
3. Large number of staff with multilingual skills; and
4. Globally located to support international call centres working on around the clock.

While telecommunications companies are big players in the e-commerce marketplace, postal and courier services are generally viewed as risking having their value being eroded as more information is shifted electronically rather than in physical form. E-commerce is having a remarkable impact on the communications industry. Telecommunications carriers have an obvious role to play in providing the communication lines and bandwidth to make network access and ultimately e-commerce possible.

Of major importance for telecommunications carriers is the impact of increasing data traffic and the use of the Internet for voice traffic. The impact of e-commerce on communications is not restricted to the telecommunication companies. Postal services are also being impacted by e-commerce. One might expect that as the sole supplier of traditional regular mail services in Australia, Australia Post would suffer a decline in the demand for its services as a result of increasing use of e-commerce. However quite the opposite has occurred—the number of items carried by Australia Post grew by 3.4 per cent last year from 4.3 billion to 4.5 billion. Even so, Australia Post is undertaking a number of strategies to find a fulfilling role in an environment of greater use of e-commerce. Australia Post is expected to launch its Internet Fulfilment System (IFS) shortly, which will move beyond simple delivery to include electronic integration of its warehousing, distribution and track and tracing capabilities for online retailers. Australia Post already delivers an average of 22 000 items from Amazon.com every monthand is the largest delivery network to 8.5 million households and businesses in Australia. IFS will enable it to compete effectively for the increased delivery of Internet-ordered products as traffic grows into the future. In addition, Australia Post will launch a web-based bill presentation and payment system, which it expects to grow to 20 million transactions by 2003 (Note: Through its network of post offices, Australia Post currently handles around 170 million bill payments annually).

Unlike online banking bill payments systems, Australia Post will offer bill presentment and will give customers the option to pay bills using accounts from more than one financial institution. Australia Post will not charge customers for using the services, instead it will charge billing principals for using the system. Consumers can pre-register with bank details and relevant information and an account ore credit card can be debited with a single mouse click.

Use of the Internet for billings, particularly for business-to-business transactions, is less expensive and more timely than traditional paper billings that use postal and courier services. The trend in electronic billings is expected to continue due to reduced transaction costs and improved service, and a greater insistence on the part of large businesses that suppliers be linked into their e-commerce systems. Use of the Internet also offers cost savings from the standardisation of technologies that have historically been incompatible, for example, for fax transmission, broadcasting and telephone circuits, though opportunities for some functions are presently constrained by bandwidth limitations. A cost saving for business generally that may affect telecommunications businesses is increased use of the Internet for selling at the expense of telephone selling and call centres. Automated selling is likely to require less labour for the selling process and for delivering after sales services, which is likely to consist of manuals and databases accessible to consumers over the Internet, with perhaps a small team of people on hand to solve difficult problems. Communications companies themselves, particularly postal and courier services, are also reducing costs as users of e-commerce services.

E-commerce in the procurement of machinery and equipment was projected to compress wholesalers' margins by 25–30 per cent over the period under consideration. Also e-commerce would increase competition and more sophisticated competition would put downward pressure on the producer's prices. E-commerce was thought to be pretty fully implemented in supply areas like fuel, so little further impact was projected.

People noted that there were conflicting trends on fuel utilisation arising from e-commerce—greater customisation meant more frequent deliveries of smaller loads, so possibly increased costs, but computer assisted routing meant that the effect was small. Telecommunications companies in the sector are incurring costs in creating new products. They are moving into e-commerce and application development and finding new value. They are moving more into Internet Protocols and data transmission. This is opening up a whole lot of new opportunities for them, especially in developing applications to suit different customer requirements, in this new environment that can mean developing software.Communications sector companies are becoming involved in new areas of business, enabled by e-commerce and new technologies. Underpinning these lines of business are new technologies.

A new technology which should have a big impact on the sector, and on business in general, is mobile e-commerce based on Wireless Access Protocol (WAP). Internet phones and Internet payment devices will also impact. One of the drivers of e-commerce is the availability of Internet devices. People are using Personal Digital Assistants more, and tapping into the existing mobile base depends on the right applications. The impact of e-commerce is different for the two main industries which comprise this sector. The telecommunications companies are big players in the e-commerce marketplace, providing many of the products and services on which e-commerce is based, as well as moving up the value chain to provide e-commerce services directly.

E-markets

Since the arrival of open access systems using the Internet, ordinary investors have also been quick to buy and sell shares electronically. Many new purely online brokers have emerged offering very low fees and several full service brokers have responded by offering online trading facilities of their own. Over 15 per cent of households in the US are reported to have conducted equity trades online. This compares with less than five per cent that bank online.

Financial markets have also been quick to adopt e-commerce and electronic trading. The Australian Stock Exchange (ASX) introduced the Stock Exchange Automated Trades System (SEATS) in 1987. Trading floors were abolished in 1990 and all trading was conducted electronically on SEATS. In 1994 the ASX introduced electronic and clearing settlement (CHESS). Reflecting continued use of e-commerce techniques, by 1999 settlement time was reduced to the trade date plus three business days. Most of what the ASX does is e-commerce, for example electronic trading of shares and executions has been occurring for 12 years.

Given this history, the ASX believe that further creation of value from e-commerce will be due to increases in speed. For example, gross settlements now take three days, but they are gearing up to handle real time settlements. In that respect it will be a new product for the ASX, and will also change the risk characteristics of trades. There is also value added by the speed of the transaction as the value of the trade can change while it is taking place. The ASX is also working with the NASDAQ to allow the joint buying and selling of shares on their indexes.

Currently, if an Australian wants to trade with NASDAQ they have to find a broker with a US affiliate or contact a broker in the US. The funds for the trade have to be raised separately. When the new service is in place, the sale of shares on one index can be used to fund the purchase of shares on the other. This service will also allow the ASX to use its IT infrastructure more intensely. Re-intermediation could also occur, with brand name labelling of shares and finance. Quicken in the US is trying to provide bundling via a portal to banks, brokers, insurance and more. The seamlessness of any new service will be important. Another factor is that new players do not have commitments to existing players that existing players have amongst themselves. The business elements of e-commerce will evolve slowly–the ASX has need of digital certification and increased reliability.Banks are keen to make greater use of Internet banking for many reasons, but a key factor is the substantial cost advantage this activity enjoys.

The Commonwealth Bank states in its 1998 Annual Report that 72 per cent of all banking transactions are conducted through electronic channels, such as telephone, the Internet, ATMs, and EFTPOS terminals. Similarly, Westpac states that around 80 per cent of their transactions are done electronically. The National Australia Bank have recently reduced the percentage of transactions through branches from 19 per cent to 14 per cent. Every customer that is to switch from a branch transaction to a lower cost channel results in a substantial saving. Competition will force the banks to pass these savings on to customers as lower fees and prices.Using the Internet for bill payment can provide savings to all parties involved including the merchant, customer and the bank. Electronic billing is likely to be a significant growth area in the economy in 2000.A flow on impact of greater use of the electronic channels and consolidation in general has been the reduction in staff required.

In order to obtain the cost savings offered by the Internet, the banking and finance sector is buying significant volumes of IT inputs. It seems likely that the major banks have raised their IT spending to accommodate a major upgrade of e-commerce requirements. It is not clear if they intend to raise spending above these levels or merely to sustain them, or indeed, if the new capital expenditure round is now complete. In order to compete in the Internet market, banks and other financial sector firms must ensure that consumers are aware of their presence in this new context.

The financial sector is the biggest spender on Internet advertising in Australia, nearly a quarter of the total spent coming from the sector. Five of the top-ten online advertisers in 1998 were from the financial services industry. The traditional concept of a branch offering all services is also changing. Banks are setting up specialist transaction centres and centres that target specific audiences.

The National Australia Bank (NAB) has 219 specialist business centres in addition to its 903 traditional branches and in Australia. The ANZ has a Business Direct Centre that offers lower priced products for smaller business with simple lending and financial service needs. There is a trend toward the use of mobile lenders and investment advisers.

Westpac have 1 000 mobile staff and during a 12 month period the Commonwealth Bank's mobile bankers conducted almost 50 000 home loan interviews, and over

24 per cent of all Commonwealth home loan approvals were generated by mobile bankers. The Commonwealth Bank has traditionally used Post Offices to provide additional branch type services for their customers. The Commonwealth plans to extend this with Woolworths Ezy Banking Westpac is working with rural communities and introducing in-store branches in pharmacies, general stores and newsagencies. Banks have traditionally provided an intermediary service of matching deposits with funding for loans.

E-commerce provides an opportunity for banks to be disintermediated from this activity. The direct provision of loans by non-banking entities such as superannuation organisations and insurance companies could be an indication of this disintermediation. Calculated from information provided in the annual reports of the National Australia Bank, Commonwealth Bank of Australia, Westpac and the Australian and New Zealand Banking Group Limited. The data does not separate out increases in branches obtained through acquisitions of overseas activities, so probably understates the fall in branches used in Australia. Traditionally banks have played an important role in the payment approval process.

The trend towards the use of credit cards (versus cheques) has had (and still does have) the potential to reduce the role of banks in the payment loop. Banks have retained some control in this area to date as the card issuing body. The move towards SET in the online payment areas will re-intermediate banks back into the online payment approval process. The likely acceptance of some form of digital cash in the future could potentially disintermediate banks again from the payment approval process.

Elimination of value is also possible in the sector. Banks now act as intermediaries in matching depositors with funds to loan applications. The function could move to brokered markets, and even to a direct market. With payments, the provision of EFTPOS enabling payments was a valuable service to bank customers.

Now with services such as Telstra's SureLink, the payment service is provided as part of a larger service. This commoditises the pure payment service. Greater use of e-commerce is also opening new opportunities in this sector. Regulatory reform, competition and the potential of the new technologies are breaking down distinctions between the roles that companies in the banking and finance sector play. E-commerce over the Internet has enabled banks to move into stock trading.

The Commonwealth Bank's ComSec is a predominantly online share trading service, although it does provide a supporting telephone service. The ANZ has recently announced an alliance with E*TRADE Australia for ANZ customers to trade securities online. There is a trend for banks to offer complete financial services to individuals and organisations. This typically includes investment advice, insurance, superannuation, share trading, and funds management. E-commerce is creating new value in the banking and finance sector.

E-commerce assists organisations in becoming virtual CFOs for small businesses by handling all financial services and providing accounts receivable and payable services. The aim is to provide a full service from operational through to strategic. For consumers, the concept is to package services around 'life events' and to provide focussed advice and services.

3

E-Insurance

Insurance helps business to stay open and individuals to continue their work or education by providing financial compensation if an insured risk occurs and causes damage. Even when no loss occurs, insurance provides peace of mind, a service of considerable, if unquantifiable, value. As a financial sector, insurance is a major investor. Life insurance can stimulate and mobilize personal savings that may, in its absence, become sterile assets. It can also relieve pressure on social welfare systems. Insurance is also needed for trade and commerce where it enhances the creditworthiness of trading partners and can reduce the risk of failure of start-ups and small and medium-sized enterprises (SMEs) as non-diversified risk-takers.

E-insurance can be broadly defined as the application of Internet and related information technologies (IT) to the production and distribution of insurance services. In a narrower sense, it can be defined as the provision of an insurance cover whereby an insurance policy is solicited, offered, negotiated and contracted online. While payment, policy delivery and claims processing may all be done online as well, technical and regulatory constraints may not allow these elements to be subject to full e-commerce application in certain countries.

However, insurance legislation worldwide is being continuously modified to accommodate online payment and policy delivery, and, outside the discussion of e-insurance metrics, these elements should be included in the narrow definition. The anticipated efficiency effect of e-insurance is twofold. First, e-insurance should reduce internal administration and management costs by automating bushiness processes, permitting real-time networking of company departments, and improving management information. Secondly, it should reduce the commissions paid to intermediaries since it can be sold directly to clients. For insurance sold to individuals, agents typically receive a commission of 10 to 15 per cent for non-life policy sales and renewals and from 35 to 100 per cent for life insurance policies in the first policy year, but much less on renewal.

However, some of the income gained in commissions that are not paid to intermediaries must be spent on online customer acquisition and marketing. Assuming cost savings do materialize, in a competitive market they would be passed on to consumers thereby allowing them to buy more insurance, or other products or services. Since insurance penetration in developing countries is only of that in developed countries, the efficiency gains created by e-insurance may contribute substantially to growth in insurance spending and thus intensify its indisputable role in promoting trade and development.

Of the $2.5 trillion worth of global insurance premiums, about 1 per cent could qualify as e-insurance, according to the broad definition. Little, if any of the premiums earned in developing countries could be described as e-insurance according to the narrow definition.

In stark contrast, the majority of the $100 billion global reinsurance business is traded using some form of electronic medium. This general assessment seems almost unchanged in comparison with previous UNCTAD reporting on e-insurance. Considered along with initial reports indicating that online premium rates are more competitive, this could point to an acceleration in online distribution of insurance covers measured by the overall value of insured assets.

During the height of the dot.com euphoria, expectations for e-insurance growth were very strong, and many insurance and reinsurance companies and intermediaries have continued to invest in their e-commerce capabilities. Swiss Re's research arm SIGMA estimates that by 2005 e-insurance will have 5 to 10 per cent market share in standardized personal lines insurance.

The corresponding figure for Europe is 3 to 5 per cent. While it is difficult to give exact figures, online sales of insurance products have been increasing steadily. Already, of the 166 million Internet users in the United States, 25 per cent use the web to find insurance information and 73 per cent of those request rate quotes. About 4 per cent of global premiums will qualify as e-insurance by 2003.

However, online premium volumes are still modest today, and this begs a number of questions. Are insurance products suitable for e-commerce? Is the insurance industry ready and willing to embrace Internet technology? Is the adoption of e-commerce practice important for insurers operating in developing countries and for their clients? How do clients benefit from purchasing insurance online and what are the pitfalls that require improved regulation?

If we can establish that the insurance product has the potential to benefit from the application of IT and e-commerce, then we can review e-insurance business and supervisory practice in a cross-comparative manner. We may find it difficult to conclude why certain e-insurance applications work and others do not. However, can we definitely exclude the fallback of unsuitability of insurance products as an explanation for modest e-commerce growth in the insurance industry?

In insurance theory, risk is often defined as the variation between actual losses and expected losses. Insurers' premium rates are based on an assessment of average expected losses and damage. However, premiums collected based on such an average rate may not be sufficient to pay for all the damages in a year, if that year generates greater-than-average losses. Thus, insurers need to have additional funds in reserve. Such reserves are established when an insurer incorporates its business and are often addressed by government insurance regulation and supervision. More importantly, reserves may be replenished during years when losses are less severe than the expected average.

There are several fundamental steps an insurer must take. First, it must calculate a premium rate for the risk it intends to insure against particular causes of damage (e.g. when insuring vehicles or homes against theft or fire). It must also establish adequate reserves to cover deviations from average, expected losses. Finally, the insurer must determine whether any particular clients are likely to attract greater than average misfortune and must decide how to adjust the rates it proposes to them individually.

As this simplified outline shows, the fundamental machinery of insurance involves mathematical treatment and statistical analysis of numerous events and the processing of large amounts of data about existing or potential clients. Not surprisingly the application of proprietary IT is widespread and has been a natural development among insurers in developed countries with competitive financial services markets.

Today, IT is widely used to handle communication with intermediaries, policy processing, premium notices, market analysis, sales forecasts, and accounting. Clearly, insurance is an information-intensive enterprise and is thus suitable for e-commerce.

The establishment of an insurance contract does not require much more than an exchange of information. As long as no damage occurs, most insurance contracts, and their performance as uninvoked promises, remain in the sphere of pure information and are therefore highly amenable to the application of IT.

Like any other contract, an insurance contract or policy needs to satisfy the four basic conditions of legality, capacity, offer and acceptance, and consideration. To ensure legality the client needs to have an insurable interest: the asset to be insured has to be the property of the client and some information confirming this is usually submitted. The requirement of capacity is satisfied by an exchange of information showing that the insurer, agent or broker is licensed and that the client is not a minor, insane, intoxicated or acting outside the scope of assigned authority.

The condition of offer and acceptance is satisfied by having the insurer offer coverage terms and conditions for an insurable interest, against a loss caused by general or named perils under particular conditions of hazard. The client reciprocates the offer by expressing an acceptance of the proposed contract. It is apparent that an enormous amount of information may be exchanged to satisfy this contract condition.

The consideration of the insurer consists of the promise of financial compensation for the loss events defined by the policy. The consideration of the client is to pay a premium. The promise is a non-physical information service. Similarly, the transfer of funds is often electronic, and even cash itself has a nominal value unrelated to its physicality. When a loss occurs, the damage is assessed and a claim is submitted. Large amounts of data are again transmitted between policyholders, intermediaries and insurers.

E-insurance requires modern e-commerce legislation that permits insurers and the insured to safely and unambiguously exchange information, make electronic payments and validate their responsibilities through digital signatures.

A frequently cited aspect of insurance that may detract from its suitability for e-commerce is that its products are often said to be "sold rather than bought". The assumption is that without the sales push of a physical agent, consumers would buy fewer and less valuable insurance policies.

Business-to-consumer (B2C) e-insurance is not considered pushy enough, and potential clients are only a mouse click away from other unrelated Internet content.

Certain issues relating to the legal and regulatory environment of a national insurance market can be overcome by having a system of physical agencies. Insurance is difficult to sell online if some or all of the following conditions exist:

— Electronic signatures are not legal;

— Credit card payment is not accepted for insurance purchases;

— Physical documents (policies) have to be delivered to clients and paper copies archived by the agent and insurer;

— Document formats are over-regulated;

— Agents and insurers have to display their license physically;

— Remuneration of insurance portals or markets is prohibited if they do not possess an agent or broker license;

— Physical proof of coverage is requested by third parties (e.g. law enforcement or estate agents).

The agency system is deeply ingrained in the insurance industry, and the insurance agent community supports the notion that insurance is sold, not bought. Insurers do not want to alienate their agents, who remain their most important sales channels. Often, insurers define the agent, not the policyholder, as their customer. It is difficult to predict whether direct Internet purchasing by consumers can replace agents.

The establishment of an insurance contract requires the exchange of large amounts of data, often of a personal nature. While the electronic medium is perfect for data transfer, consumers often worry about the extent to which information submitted by them will be kept private, both at the time of contracting and in the future. When submitting data to an agent, clients assume that they can hold the agent responsible and can seek legal remedy if their privacy is transgressed. The anonymous nature of a website can provoke the opposite assumption in that behind the monitor there is nobody to hold responsible. Clients may also suffer data fatigue when filling out lengthy online forms and may, as a result, give up on soliciting a quote without the coaching of an agent.

Thus, many insurers have opted to provide only policy information and insurance education on their websites and leave the actual selling to intermediaries. When clients decide to ask for a quote, they are asked for their postal or zip code and are directed to a nearby agent. The problem with this strategy is that insurance agents may not be highly regarded by consumers for their professional honesty and ethics. In the United States, Gallup polls conducted yearly from 1993 to 2000 ranked insurance agents at the very bottom of the credibility scale. Only 9 to 12 per cent of respondents gave insurance agents very high or high marks for honesty and ethics, in comparison with 25 to 37 per cent for bankers and 13 to 19 per cent for stockbrokers, in consecutive polls during the same period. Consumers may be dealing with insurance agents purely for a lack of a better option. This may be their destiny in developing countries for the foreseeable future due to relatively low levels of Internet and credit card penetration.

The modest progress in e-insurance, in developed countries, compared to the online banking sector, can also be explained by the notion that insurance companies consider the use of e-commerce, and its disintermediating effect, a fairly risky business strategy.

A recent Swiss Re SIGMA report on e-insurance concluded that "re-engineering traditional business processes is expensive and often meets with considerable opposition from within the (insurance) company itself." A similar report by CSFB pointed out that "legacy systems are inflexible and expensive to change... the (insurance) culture is understandably risk averse... (while) the Internet threatens existing distribution systems, creating a thorny channel conflict."

A recent survey by KMPG revealed that, while the industry is planning and preparing for e-insurance, for 40 per cent of companies e-business actually a threat because of a lack of strategic vision. Further, a quarter of the 175 insurance executives interviewed affirmed that their companies lacked e-business competencies.

In a recent joint study by the Economist Intelligence Unit and PricewaterhouseCoopers, two-thirds of the insurance managers interviewed said that their own companies do not have sufficient e-business leadership capabilities for success in e-insurance.

The same study noted that few insurers believed they had the requisite in-house technological skills for e-business. It is worth noting that, that while insurers employ on average 48 per cent more IT staff than banks do, the majority are used to service and manage unique proprietary IT systems where it is difficult to achieve economies of scale.

Insurance consumers may find certain products difficult to understand and may be hesitant to buy online. However, the research cited indicates that insurers have not yet found a way to put the "e" into insurance. Results in banking, stock broking and tourism show that the online consumer in developed countries has the technology and willingness to engage in e-commerce.

There are ongoing debates about the suitability of individual insurance product for e-commerce. The conventional wisdom is that obligatory, very simple or low-price products do not require a seller's push and thus can be distributed through e-commerce. The greatest demand is for motor vehicle insurance, followed by health, homeowner's and term life insurance.

In line with the general relationship, insurers selling online directly to clients are offering a very restricted portfolio of products. Progressive. com, a leader in the United States online insurance market, is currently offering only motor vehicle insurance and related products.

Another prominent online insurer, Allstate.com, is more ambitious and offers motor, homeowner's, life and small business insurance policies. Amica.com provides only motor and homeowner's policies, and several types of life insurance. European insurers also vary in the scope of offered insurance policies. For example, Ineas.com provides motor vehicle, homeowner's and accident insurance while esure.com offers only motor vehicle insurance.

While many insurers continue to rely on their agency networks and cling to the "sold not bought" paradigm, there is little real evidence supporting it, apart from pronouncements about its genuineness that are often articulated by insurance agents and managers. What is needed to bring insurance online is the implementation of best-practice management and technology suited to e-commerce.

Internet and e-commerce technologies are already changing the structure of the insurance industry. The pre-Internet insurance world is largely linear, with individuals (personal lines) or businesses (commercial lines) moving risk to insurers, sometimes directly, but more often through the intermediation of brokers and agents. Intermediaries are responsible for processing more than 90 per cent of all premiums collected.

The main characteristics of an internet-enabled insurance industry and market are that technology can be evenly distributed and information intermediation is no longer a necessity but a preference. Gone is the linear travel of payments and risk information from client to (re)insurer. Buyers of personal and commercial insurance and reinsurance can choose to pursue multiple paths to acquire price and policy information.

Insurers and reinsurers have extended their reach through their online incarnations. Brokers and agents may do so as well. They were an irreplaceable link in the pre-Internet insurance industry. Agents intermediated sales of policies to non-businesses, such as personal life insurance, motor vehicle insurance, homeowners insurance and various savings and investment schemes. They also intermediated insurance for small and medium-sized business.

Brokers intermediated insurance between large organizations, or businesses, and insurers, as well as between insurers and reinsurers. Their economic role was to enhance market efficiency by diminishing information asymmetries between buyers and sellers caused by any of the following situations:

1. The insurer is not fully informed of the scope of the demand, or the insured is not knowledgeable about the selection of insurance policies and prices available; or
2. The insurer has not fully mastered the technical and economic details of the proposed risk, or the insured does not clearly understand the insurance policy's proposed terms and conditions.

In practice, agents are generally authorized to sell policies from only one or a few insurers. Further, the terms and policy wordings of different insurers, even if distributed by the same agent, often do not match. To clarify these differences and enable cross-comparisons is perhaps the most important role of the agent.

The obvious question is: can Internet and e-commerce technologies do better than the physical agent-broker system at improving market transparency and competitiveness and educating consumers and insurers about policy and risk technicalities? The answer is a qualified yes.

Online buyers compare a wide range of prices and policy conditions for a particular type of policy and then choose the lowest priced product. In theory, this practice should cause overall price decreases in specific insurance product categories. Early research suggests that the price of term life insurance in the United States fell 8 to 15 per cent in the late 1990s, a drop attributable to increasing Internet use by prospecting clients.

Insurance companies selling online can, on their end, exploit cost efficiencies arising from the application of IT in production or distribution and pass these savings on to consumers, while still staying profitable.

However, research on the relationship between e-commerce and prices is still limited, and the notion that the Internet makes insurance, or any other service or product, cheaper and influences its market to be more competitive should not be treated as an axiom. For example, the ease of price discovery may equally help sellers collude in price fixing.

Further, promoting brand names and advertising online services, combined with investments in technology, imposes high fixed operating costs and can lead to market concentration and an overall decrease in competitiveness.

Sellers may also pursue different strategies to decrease market homogeneity, from bundling products with "free" services and promoting loyalty schemes, or locking-in clients by offering policy upgrades. Finally, the Internet enables insurers to conduct client profiling and discover their lifestyle and Internet habits, which may push the information balance back in favour of the insurer.

E-insurance cannot happen if clients, intermediaries and insurers cannot exchange policy data in a meaningful and standardized way. Pre-Internet proprietary IT systems were unique to particular insurers and their agency network. Reincarnating these systems on the Internet requires establishing broadly accepted and public data definitions and standards. A key technology is XML (extensible markup language), which provides a way of labelling data so that they can be exchanged online in a coherent and meaningful way.

Personal lines insurance refers to coverage bought by individuals such as motor vehicle insurance, property insurance, personal liability cover, and health and life insurance. In the pre-Internet scenario, personal lines occupy the least IT-intensive area and are therefore subject to the greatest disruption from the introduction of e-commerce technologies. The disruption level is further increased by the intensity of agents' intermediation in these insurance lines.

However modest the progress, many insurers see e-commerce, and its disintermediating effects, as a source of increased competitiveness. This judgement has affected the expectations within the agents community. As a counter-strategy, many physical agents see their future in improving their e-commerce capacities vis-à-vis the carriers they serve. Examples of pro-agent IT providers are Applied Systems and Doris Inc..

Insurers are wary of alienating their agents. In a recent survey in the United States, the majority of insurers confirmed that they were "focusing their technological efforts on upgrading outdated IT infrastructure that strengthens the independent agent distribution channel."

The same survey found that only 15 per cent of insurance carriers practiced e-insurance, broadly defined. Among agents there is a similar, if not identical, approach. The majority of agents in the United States use the Internet to communicate with insurers, while only 15 per cent use it to generate leads that may bring new business.

An UNCTAD analysis in 2000 suggested that the growth of e-insurance would not meet expectations if insurers focused their investment on marketing, customer support and support of intermediaries rather than on establishing Internet sales.

Whereas many insurers have extensive internal IT applications, policy and client data are not easily accessed outside the physical confines of the company office. Such introverted IT systems have been made possible by the agency distribution system, which has insulated insurers from their policy-holding clients. At the same time, insulated IT has satisfied the need for security, an important consideration since insurers use clients' private and personal data in everyday business.

It is interesting to note that more than 50 per cent of agents do not have real-time connectivity with their insurers. In fact, the physical agency system addresses what is perhaps the greatest weakness of online insurance distribution: the low frequency of website repeat visits. Typically, once a policy is contracted online, the policyholder sees little reason to periodically check the insurer's site: there is little or no account activity between policy renewals, unless the policyholder acquires new assets needing coverage, or submits a claim. A client's contact with an agent for policy renewals is seen as an opportunity to push and sell other insurance products. However, it may well turn out that banks, not the e-insurer, are the insurance agents' worst enemy.

In countries where banks are licensed to sell personal insurance products, insurers and their agents may be under threat. While clients renew insurance policies yearly, they typically check their bank accounts, offline and online, on a daily or weekly basis, thus providing opportunities for banks to promote their own insurance and investment products.

To compete successfully for attention online, insurers and agents must provide clients with reasons to visit their sites. The content should reflect the clients' or communities' interests and lifestyle, as determined by an analysis of data submitted by policyholders for insurance purposes.

However, such analysis may raise legal concerns, as policy data is submitted for specific and restricted purposes and often may not be used otherwise. Where regulations permit, insurers may explore offering financial products related to mortgages, investments and financing of motor vehicles and durable goods.

In developing countries, the issue of disintermediation in the personal lines business will become critical when access to and use of the Internet, credit cards and other means of online payment increase significantly.

As in developed countries, in many developing countries clients do not hold the agency system in high regard. When online insurance and bancassurance become a real alternative, one can expect a decrease in agency-based delivery of insurance products.

Monitoring national and regional Internet user and financial demographics can help insurers in developing countries predict when and how to move in becoming a competitive online player. Even where the figures do not necessarily justify investing in a full-blown e-commerce infrastructure, it is advantageous for all insurers to have a web presence with the following components:

— Corporate and financial information;
— Insurance education and awareness building;
— FAQs;
— Product descriptions;
— Examples of typical policies and prices;
— Contact information;
— A functioning e-mail help desk; and
— Agent locators.

An UNCTAD survey of 249 insurers in Africa found that only 54 had websites. Of these 42 provided insurance and policy information. The rest provided only basic company information and contact details. Twenty-nine insurers had e-mail addresses, but very few seemed to be functional. While this is a start, even considering the underdeveloped IT infrastructure, there is much room for growth in Internet presence.

Insurers in developing countries should not assume that establishing a basic Internet functionality constitutes an e-commerce strategy or presence. When the time comes to adopt a more intense Internet and e-commerce practice, insurers may find their operational business process IT system out of date or underdeveloped and may be unable to interface it with their website. This problem has been recognized by UNCTAD which, to help remedy such deficiencies, is cooperating with the AIO in developing operational insurance software tailored for small and medium-size insurers in Africa.

The main threat to insurers in developing countries may come from foreign insurers incorporating locally that have substantial IT budgets and international and regional experience in transplanting their IT solutions. Companies like John Hancock, AIG, Manulife Financial, Prudential Financial, ING and New York Life International have made forays into a number of developing countries. However, implementing IT and e-commerce technology is never a goal in itself. AIG has suggested that it would not implement an IT-based processing solution in a developing country if it were cheaper to hire people to do manual processing.

A further issue for insurers in developing countries is the use of business process outsourcing (BPO) by global insurers. Hartford Life has been transferring operations to Argentina, while MetLife has established partnerships to outsource business processes to India. Prudential has been outsourcing to Barbados and India for a number of years. This indicates that, as far as e-readiness is concerned, the human resources needed for e-insurance are within reach in a number of developing countries.

Buyers of commercial insurance often require tailored underwriting as many of them are large businesses operating in multiple locations with varying degrees of hazard, or running sophisticated industrial systems. Companies with significant assets normally set up their own risk management departments. These departments are knowledgeable about the risk profiles and exposures of their business and are indispensable in coverage negotiations.

Due to the size and complexity of commercial risks, few insurers have made progress in offering commercial lines insurance via the Internet. In a recent survey conducted by the fifth largest workers' compensation insurer in the United States, Kemper Insurance, not one of the surveyed SME businesses said it would buy commercial insurance online.

A similar study by IVANS, a U.S. insurance e-business integrator, found that only 4 per cent of small businesses would definitely buy insurance online, while 51 per cent are interested in using the Internet to research insurance products. One of the largest global financial companies and insurers, AIG promotes its commercial insurance activities online but does not actually give quotes. After requesting existing policy information that may be submitted online, AIG follows up with a response from a particular expert or department.

An important reason for the relatively minor role of e-insurance for commercial lines is that large businesses do not consider the transfer of risk to an insurer by way of a policy to be the only or even the primary motivation for purchasing insurance. A recent study suggests that a "company's purchase of insurance is intended to introduce the external monitoring role of the insurance underwriter, hence inhibiting opportunistic behaviour on part of the company and so enhancing the degree of cooperation among stakeholders and reducing transaction costs."

Large companies may choose to do business with insurers even when they have the financial capacity to self-insure in order to have the insurer as a neutral advisor. Further, insuring own assets with own capital may be imprudent in cases of catastrophic risks. Finally, a company's stake- or shareholders may look askance at the insured's diversification into insurance underwriting through self-insurance. Investors can always diversify their portfolios on the securities markets, should they wish to do so.

For all these reasons, commercial lines e-insurance may eventually face the challenge of providing intelligent online risk management consultancy. However, in the near future, its scope may be limited to providing contact and product information and generating leads.

The application of IT in reinsurance has traditionally been intense, both internally and among reinsurers and reinsurance brokers. The three original European networks, Limnet, Rinet and WIN, and Joint Venture merged in 1999 and operated until November 2001 under the name WISe (Worldwide Insurance Electronic Commerce).

Before the merger, Limnet estimated that, among its members, 15 per cent of all risks were being handled electronically as opposed to 90 per cent of claims. Rinet estimated that 60 per cent of world and 80 per cent of European reinsurance income was transacted through its network, as well as 50 per cent of United States gross reinsurance premium income.

In addition to its basic mission to develop e-commerce solutions for insurers, WISe was involved in developing e-insurance data standards through its Joint Venture activities. In October 2001, WISe merged its standard-setting activities with ACORD. As a result ACORD has become the de facto global e-commerce standards body for insurance. WISe's commercial activities have since been acquired by Ins-sure, which provides the London insurance market and European insurers with electronic business processing, policy administration, premium and claim settlement services.

Reinsurance is rapidly coming online. While examples abound, approaches vary. Certain companies are marketing and distributing their own reinsurance products on their websites. Others have engaged in cooperative strategies and are attempting to set up reinsurance markets or exchanges. The world's second largest rein-surer, Swiss Re, debuted in 2000 with an online reinsurance capacity auction system called Elrix. Today, all of its efforts have been thrown behind inreon.com, a joint venture with Munich Re, another global insurance giant.

Other e-market-based or exchange platforms include RI3K, backed by BRIT Insurance Ltd. and assisted by AXA and Citibank; UniRisX, backed by the technology company Unisys and the reinsurance broker Price Forbes; and E-Reinsurer, backed by Chubb. RI3K intends to use the 2002 reinsurance renewals as a test, when it would trade a designated $100 million. Other prominent reinsurers, such as Frankona GE, St.Paul and AXA-ACS, are developing company-specific e-commerce platforms as well.

The essence of the debate in the reinsurance sector is which will prevail: the reinsurance e-markets or the individual reinsurance company portals. While it is too early to judge, the following list of the pros and cons of reinsurance e-markets may give some guidance:

Pros

— Buyers get access to multiple quotes from several reinsurers;

— Capacity can be larger;

Cons

— Few players are fully committed, many are developing own solutions in tandem;

— Standardized products may not satisfy buyers' needs;

— Aside from reinsurers, e-markets need to attract brokers and cedants.

Proprietary reinsurance portals or markets that meet the narrow definition of e-insurance may not be trading more than 1 per cent of global reinsurance premiums by the end of 2002. However, because reinsurers have been operating in an IT-enabled environment for almost two decades, e-insurance is expected to catch on quickly. The fact that reinsurers' clients are ceding insurers and brokers (i.e. insurance professionals) may hasten the adoption of e-commerce in reinsurance.

The implications for developing countries will become material when reinsurance markets and exchanges start trading a significant part of global reinsurance premiums. Developing-country insurers will be expected to work with the e-insurance infrastructure being set up by the market leaders; failing to do so will increase the risk of technological marginalization and may also increase their costs of reinsurance cession and acceptance. There is a need to anticipate these developments and be prepared.

In the insurance context, the main application for m-insurance (insurance using m-commerce methods) will probably be in enhancing the performance of the field agent or employee. Wireless devices will enable field staffers to access data resources that will enhance distribution, improve cross-selling, and appreciably speed up loss assessment, claims submissions and reimbursements.

Attitudes to m-insurance vary in line with the general acceptance level of m-commerce technology. In Japan, where wireless communications have made significant progress, the Tokio Marine & Fire Insurance

Company has a fully developed m-system. Agents use mobile devices to access the company's Intranet to source quotes, and for e-mail communication. *New York Life* is also preparing a mobile initiative for implementation in Asia. A mobile strategy for insurance agents in developing countries may be a workable proposition especially since it does not necessarily have to be related to a sales oriented e-commerce strategy. The objective is to increase agents' efficiency and enhance their ability to close a contract.

While many insurance carriers in the developed world are concerned about how to bring their proprietary/ legacy computer systems online, many insurers in developing countries are still working with paper-form-based administration systems. They are motivated to start building company IT infrastructures for three reasons:

1. Markets are liberalizing, and competitive pressures are forcing insurers to increase productivity and efficiency;
2. Their counterparts in developed countries require Internet-based electronic data interchange for ceding or accepting reinsurance;
3. Any prospective e-commerce strategy needs back-office IT that can communicate with an Internet-based front end or website.

While many IT companies in developed countries produce software for the insurance business, developing countries need not necessarily look very far for suppliers. An interesting example is Infosys, an IT services and consulting company from Bangalore, India. Aetna, Aon Corporation, AXA Online Japan, Fairfax Financial

Services, Marsh Canada, New York Life, SunAmerica, Suncorp Metway and Swiss Re have all been listed as insurance clients on the Infosys website.

In its most recent collaboration with Northwestern Mutual Life Insurance, Infosys has developed an online funds transfer option for variable life and annuity policyholders. Customers can now log on and make immediate transfers from their accounts, thus eliminating potential delays associated with processing allocation change and asset transfer requests.

While a number of off-the-shelf products are available in developed countries, due to the differing operating standards and national regulatory principles, it is no easy task to find an application that works out of the box. Having reviewed the possibilities, the African Insurance Organization and UNCTAD have established a project to produce a fully functional software application for SME African insurance companies.

Middleware is a general term for software that provides an interface for two separate and usually already existing software applications. For example, middle-ware is often used to enable two or more distinct data-bases to exchange data. The movement in the insurance industry from proprietary IT systems to Internet-based IT and e-business applications for e-insurance may require extensive and robust middleware applications.

Apart from e-insurance, mergers and acquisitions and the globalization of the financial services industry also support the demand for middleware. The speed of e-insurance adoption may also depend on how much support integration middleware developers show for the adoption of XML for data transformation, exchange and integration. Those developers that can provide solutions for integrating existing or legacy systems while ensuring that users can easily and cost-effectively transform data between other data formats and XML using Acord standards may have a competitive advantage.

The development of e-commerce, particularly on the Internet, presents new challenges and concerns for insurance regulators and supervisors from developed, as well as developing countries. The establishment of Internet-based insurance businesses offers both individual insurance consumers and insurers and intermediaries potential efficiency and cost benefits.

E-insurance improves information symmetry and market transparency conditions and may enhance competition that can lead to reduced prices. For insurance regulators from developing countries, Internet-based supervisory tools may increase efficiency by streamlining and speeding up reporting from insurance enterprises.

The possibilities offered by Internet communication can also greatly improve the delivery of information to the public, insurers and local and international investors regarding market conditions, rights and obligations. Also, secure Internet communication could be a major tool for fostering international cooperation among regulators to improve the security of insurance markets.

From the perspective of a supervisory authority in a developing country, major concerns pertaining to e-insurance relate to cross-border activities and how to safeguard the interests of consumers if they contract policies in other jurisdictions. However, as most countries continue to require local licensing for insurers offering products in the domestic market and prohibit cross-border activity, cross-border trade in personal lines and mass insurance products has not expanded. Also, the cost of establishing e-insurance platforms, along with related marketing costs, has deterred financially unsound operators from establishing a significant web presence.

E-insurance provides a new channel for distributing insurance products that accelerates transaction processes, creating more opportunities for fraud. It imposes on supervisors the burden of developing supervision methods that permit quick responses to threats to the interests of insurance consumers. However, the emergence of e-insurance does not fundamentally alter the principles on which today's insurance supervision is based.

For regulators, the essential question relating to e-insurance, as well as to other distribution methods, is how to protect insurance consumers. Supervisors have therefore approached e-insurance operations in the same way they supervise business and market of traditional insurance operations, including rate monitoring, surveying the marketing of insurance products, responding to public complaints, conducting consumer education and fraud monitoring.

To tackle the particularities of e-insurance supervision, the International Association of Insurance Supervisors (IAIS) established a working group on e-commerce and the Internet. This working group has issued "The Principles on the Supervision of Insurance Activities on the Internet" that were approved by the IAIS at its annual conference in Cape Town on 10 October 2000.

More generally, insurance supervisory authorities have the same concerns as those regulating other e-businesses, particularly e-finance businesses: business continuity, personal data privacy, payment procedures and security, electronic signatures and IT platforms.

E-insurance was once perceived as a distribution channel that would erase national boundaries, since a single e-insurance platform established in one jurisdiction could offer insurance services globally. This has not occurred, since in most countries the establishment of a locally licensed business is required before insurance services can be offered to domestic consumers.

E-insurance platforms thus fall under the laws and regulations of the respective jurisdictions where services are offered. More precisely, existing regulations relating to market conduct determine how insurance providers may conduct their business online. Competition rules and transparency and information requirements form the core of market conduct regulations. Monitoring of rates, marketing of insurance products, handling of public complaints, consumer education and fraud are areas included under this aspect of supervision.

In many developing countries, insurers are required to file rates, terms, conditions and contractual documentation for approval by supervisory authorities before the underlying product is offered to the public. E-insurance offerings too, are governed by such requirements.

Often minimum and maximum rates are established for compulsory individual insurance products such as motor vehicle insurance, workmen's compensation and some fire exposures. This is making it difficult for e-insurance operators to undercut prices offered by traditional competitors. Supervisory authorities should pay particular attention to the terms, conditions and contractual documentation that are presented on insurance providers' websites. The supervisory authority should ensure that the contractual relationships have a legal basis that is not prejudicial to the interests of the insured, since the insured does not generally participate in the negotiations relating to policy clauses.

In the case of life insurance, supervisors should require that certain clauses be contained in the policies published on websites. This includes clauses such as incontestability, under which the insurer, after a certain period, can no longer contest statements made by applicants. Also, a clause on nonforfeiture should be shown. Such a clause protects the cash value of the policy and provides for a grace period after the premium is due, during which the policy cannot lapse. Such a clause is particularly pertinent for Internet transactions where contracting and payment cannot occur at the same time.

In the developing country context, because of a general lack of insurance education and in order to allow consumers to make informed decisions, a large degree of comparability between contracts offered over the web should be maintained during the initial phase of establishing e-insurance operations. Two other problems to be addressed are that

(a) because of different hardware and software configurations, information presented on the web may look different to different viewers, and

(b) computer proficiency may lead to an unintended contractual result.

Certain guidelines regulating basic website content may be needed: for example, companies could be required to inform who is the supervising body and who are the final risk carriers in the cases where purchases are made from an agent's or broker's website.

Electronic signatures are important not only to confirm the existence of a contract but also for specifying the starting date of the purchased insurance coverage. The validity and effectiveness of a contract may be influenced by failures in data transmission.

A consumer may be under the impression that a contract is in place, while the insurer may have received corrupted data that does not allow a policy to be issued. The existence of a problem may not be obvious until the insured attempts to make claim under the nonexistent policy. Also, after a policy takes effect, it may be necessary to cancel, change or complement it.

Possible reasons for such an intervention include the discovery of an error or a fundamental change in the insured's risk profile. In such a case, it may be prudent to ask whether online insurance products should carry a "return or exchange of goods policy" and what kind of security is needed to prevent accidental or unauthorized cancellation.

Also, supervisors should determine whether an insurer posting offerings on the Internet is discriminating against certain categories of consumers. The traditional roles of supervisors - to ensure that compulsory mass products or personal lines are affordable and available, and to ensure the fair treatment of consumers - should be maintained with regard to products offered on the Internet.

Supervisory bodies should preserve the fairness of information presented to consumers and should attentively monitor the marketing of e-insurance products. Advertisements should not be misleading, past experience should not be used to predict future results, and products should not misrepresent benefits. Often insurers differentiate their products from those of competitors by inaccurately describing or overstating advantages and benefits.

When an intermediary offers insurance products over the Internet, such a seller should be required to obtain a license before establishing a presence on the web. The licensing procedure should require the intermediary to undergo competence tests, and the its e-insurance platform and website should be screened in the same way as those established by insurers.

Supervisors and regulators typically maintain that sales over the Internet increase opportunities for insurance fraud, money laundering and the misselling of insurance products. Some criminal groups engage in mass subscription of single policies under false or given identities, redeeming the policies quickly thereafter in order to launder money.

As no direct contact is established between parties to an insurance contract established via the Internet, e-insurance is an obvious target for money laundering operations. Supervisors should ensure that e-insurance providers have sound mechanisms in place for authenticating the identity of policyholders. Also, to trace unsound or fraudulent operators and consumers, it is paramount that supervisory authorities establish communication networks among themselves to share information on such perpetrators.

E-insurance, like other e-finance businesses, is at risk from both internal and external security threats (infiltration, corruption and theft of customer data files).

Increased connectivity, in particular the connection of internal networks with the Internet, introduces new vulnerabilities that require the deployment of more advanced and effective security tools.

Regulators should take steps to ensure that e-insurance providers have the necessary security in place to protect the integrity of information and the privacy and confidentiality of policyholders' data, whether the data storage is performed by the e-insurance provider or outsourced to Internet service providers.

Internet-based reporting and monitoring of public complaints could prove an indispensable tool for insurance supervisors. In a number of countries, formal offices within the supervisory authority have been established to respond to insurance customers' complaints. Their purpose is to streamline administrative procedures and sometimes to serve as an alternative to judiciary proceedings.

For supervisors, the monitoring of complaints provides a very useful source of information for holding insurers responsible for their offered services. To resolve complaints, supervisors should facilitate communication between insurers and complaining customers. They should make sure that companies have complied with the law and have responded promptly and fairly, and they should inform insurers of problems that customers experience with contract language, customer service or technical aspects of the website. Also, websites posting insurance offerings should give contact information for the official authority dealing with consumer complaints, and the site should clearly describe the mechanism for dispute settlement. One of the simplest and most useful Internet tools is the FAQ (frequently asked questions) page. A well-structured, comprehensive and easily navigable FAQ page can satisfy the vast majority of public queries.

To build consumer's awareness and understanding of insurance and to improve market efficiency, consumer education is paramount. E-insurance offerings should include educational material to help consumers understand the products they buy. Also, supervisory authorities should provide guidance and educational material on their websites for consumers interested in purchasing insurance online. Insurance laws, regulations and statistics can be made more easily and widely accessible through the Internet. Most Latin American and Asian as well as many African and Central and Eastern European insurance supervisory authorities have already established websites designed to inform the public.

The advantages that the electronic format offers for compiling and processing data allow supervisors to devote more time and resources to analysing periodic financial reporting by insurers. Many supervisors in developing and emerging markets have dedicated websites for the submission and processing of reporting from insurance companies, and several have developed Internet-based solutions.

The Egyptian Insurance Supervisory Authority is offering a financial reporting application, on a cooperative basis to its counterparts in other African countries. Whenever an insurance provider establishes an e-insurance operation in a country, a continuous dialogue should be established between the e-insurer and the regulatory body to resolve areas of uncertainty before the operation is launched, and to contribute to regulatory development. Authorities should continually adapt their insurance legislation to the needs of their insurance consumers, taking into account shifting consumer interests.

Among factors that have inhibited the development of cross-border e-insurance are the wide variations regulatory and supervisory requirements between national and state jurisdictions. If an e-insurance operator wants to offer services in several jurisdictions, it needs to undergo obtain licenses and comply with the respective jurisdictions' supervisory, tax and other authorities. It may be difficult to incorporate all the different and sometimes contradictory requirements into a single e-insurance platform.

Recent studies have concluded that the actual differences between national approaches are so extensive that e-insurers are unlikely to do business on a multi-country basis in the near future. A more likely development would be increased targeted penetration of national markets, with whose regulatory and supervisory requirements e-insurers are familiar.

To avoid being indicted by a national supervisory authority for unlawfully offering insurance services in that national market, e-insurers should clearly indicate on their website their identity (address, home country) and the jurisdictions in which they are legally permitted to provide insurance services. Also, e-insurance providers should post strong specific disclaimers and risk warnings directed to citizens of countries where the e-insurer is not authorized to operate.

The home country supervisory authority should oblige e-insurers to post such disclaimers and warnings. The growth of cross-border e-insurance will necessitate a harmonization of regulatory and supervisory frameworks, the recognition by insurers of home country regulators and of home country complaints and dispute settlement mechanisms. Thus it will require extensive cooperation between regulatory bodies around the world. Such developments could be part of international negotiations on the opening of national financial markets such as those conducted under the aegis of the World Trade Organization.

4

Unleashing Human Creativity

Today's technological transformations hinge on each country's ability to unleash the creativity of its people, enabling them to understand and master technology, to innovate and to adapt technology to their own needs and opportunities. Nurturing creativity requires flexible, competitive, dynamic economic environments.

For most developing countries this means building on reforms that emphasize openness -to new ideas, new products and new investments. But at the heart of nurturing creativity is expanding human skills. For that reason, technological change dramatically raises the premium every country should place on investing in the education and skills of its people.

Many developing countries are in a good position to exploit the opportunities of the technology revolution and advance human development. Others face significant hurdles, lacking the kind of economic environment that encourages innovation, lacking the skills and institutions to adapt new technologies to local needs and constraints. But sound public policy can make a difference. The key is to create an environment that mobilizes people 's creative potential to use and develop technological innovations.

Creating an environment that encourages innovation requires political and macroeconomic stability. Take the Asian success stories, built on a strong commitment to education and health coupled with low inflation, moderate fiscal and balance of payments deficits and high levels of savings and investment. It is not just big firms that demand stability.

Small businesses and family farms also depend on a stable financial setting where savings are safe and borrowing is possible. And they are where innovation and adaptation often start. While such stability is necessary, it is not enough. Proactive policies are required to stimulate innovation.

Technology policy can help to create a common understanding among key actors about the centrality of technology to economic diversification. Reforms to make telecommunications competitive are vital for giving people and organizations better access to information and communications technology.

To stimulate technology-oriented research, governments can promote links between universities and industry -and provide fiscal incentives for private firms to conduct research and development. Stimulating entrepreneurship is also essential, and venture capital can be important in fostering technology-based start-up businesses.

Governments need to establish a broad technology strategy in partnership with all key stake-holders. Several governments have promoted technology development directly. Some have subsidized high-technology industries -with industrial policies that have been widely criticized because government does not always do a good job of picking winners.

But what government can do is identify areas where coordination will make a difference because no private investor will act alone -say, in building infrastructure. Here, some governments have done a credible job.

Many countries are conducting "foresight studies "to create more coherent science and technology policy and to identify future demands and challenges, linking science and technology policy to economic and social needs. The process creates awareness among stakeholders about the state of technological activity in the country, emerging trends worldwide and the implications for national priorities and competitiveness.

Involving civil society in areas relating to new technological developments with potentially strong social and environmental impacts helps build consensus on a response. India, the Republic of Korea, South Africa, Thailand and several Latin American countries are now involved in such exercises.

In the United Kingdom the exercise has led to resource allocations and incentives to promote new technologies in a mature economy. Governments have not always led the process.

In Costa Rica businesses took the lead in the effort that led to Intel's decision to invest there. Costa Rica was able to attract technology-intensive foreign direct investment because of its social and political stability, its proximity to the United States and its highly skilled labour force, built up through decades of emphasis on education.

Telecommunications and Internet costs are particularly high in developing countries. Monthly Internet access charges amount to 1.2% of average monthly income for a typical US user, compared with 614% in Madagascar, 278% in Nepal, 191% in Bangladesh and 60% in Sri Lanka. With high costs and low incomes, community access is key to Internet diffusion in much of the developing world.

Computers, email accounts and Internet connections are often shared by several individuals or households. Telecentres, Internet kiosks and community learning centres make telephones, computers and the Internet more accessible and more affordable for more people.

In the United Republic of Tanzania Adesemi Communications International is providing the first reliable telephone service. It has installed durable, user-friendly units capable of connecting local, long-distance and international calls. The company 's wireless system allows the flexibility to install payphones where they are most needed, regardless of whether landlines exist. Small businesses dependent on communications have reaped tremendous benefits.

In Peru Red Cientifica Peruana, the largest provider of Internet access in the country, has set up a national network of 27 telecentres. A big part of the reason for the high costs is that most countries have had state monopolies for telecommunications services.

The UK technology foresight programme, announced in 1993, is forging a closer partnership between scientists and industrialists to guide publicly financed science and technology activity. More market oriented and less science driven than similar efforts elsewhere, the programme has had three phases. First it set up 15 panels of experts on the markets and technologies of interest to the country, each chaired by a senior industrialist. Each panel was charged with developing future scenarios for its area of focus, identifying key trends and suggesting ways to respond. In 1995 the panels reported to a steering group, which synthesized the main findings and identified national priorities.

Next the steering group produced a report distilling its recommendations under six themes: social trends and impacts of new technologies; communications and computing; genes and new organisms, processes and products; new materials, synthesis and processing; precision and control in management, automation and process engineering; and environmental issues.

The steering group assigned priorities to three categories: key technology areas, where further work was vital; intermediate areas, where efforts needed to be strengthened; and emerging areas, where work could be considered if market opportunities were promising and world-class capabilities could be developed.

For example, research in the four priority areas - nanotechnology, mobile wireless communications, biomaterials and sustainable energy -is being supported through a research award scheme. Another example is its application in Scotland. Scottish Enterprise hosts the Scottish foresight coordinator, who focuses on promoting foresight as a tool for business to think about and respond to future change in a structured way.

The coordinator works with a wide range of public, private and academic actors. While a key goal is to help individual companies better manage change, this is being achieved by channelling efforts through a range of trusted business intermediaries -industry bodies, networks and local delivery organizations -that have a sustainable influence on company activities.

On education and skills, the ethos of the foresight programme is captured in one of its statements: "The roots of our learning systems -classrooms and lecture theatres -can be traced back to the needs of the 19th century industrial age. At the start of the 21st century we need to re-engineer the learning process.

While many existing educational institutions will remain, they will look very different to those of today. They will become more social environments in which to support effective learning, and will perform new functions and have different responsibilities."

The new export promotion model was supported from the beginning by the Costa Rica Investment and Development Board (CINDE), a private non-profit organization founded in 1983 by prominent business people, supported by the government and financed by donor grants. Its broad aim was to promote economic development, but attracting foreign direct investment was always a top priority.

In the early 1990s CINDE realized that the country was losing competitiveness in industries relying on unskilled labour and that the North American Free Trade Agreement (NAFTA) would give Mexico better access to the US market. So it decided to focus its efforts to attract investment only on sectors that were a good match for Costa Rica's relatively high education levels. It chose electronics and related activities, rapidly growing industries that required skilled labour.

Meantime, Intel was starting to look for a site for a chip assembly and testing plant. CINDE campaigned for Costa Rica, and in 1996 Intel decided to locate its plant there. Four factors were key:

Costa Rica had political and social stability, the rule of law and a low level of corruption; relatively liberal rules relating to international trade and capital flows; a relatively well-educated and technically skilled but low-cost workforce with acceptable knowledge of English; a "pro-business "environment with a favourable attitude towards foreign direct investment; a good package of incentives; and good location and transportation logistics.

The country's growing emphasis on attracting high-technology foreign direct investment gave credibility to the case that it had the human resources Intel required.

An aggressive, effective and knowledgeable foreign investment promotion agency (CINDE), with links to the government, arranged successful meetings between Intel executives and public authorities.

The government understood the importance of an Intel investment in the country. The president met with Intel executives and encouraged the rest of the government to help Intel.

Intel's investment has had a big impact on Costa Rica's ability to attract other foreign direct investment in high-technology industries-and on the economy's general competitiveness in skill-intensive industries. Intel's reputation for rigorous site selection has given other companies the confidence to invest in the country.

Intel has also contributed by training its own workforce and supporting universities. The Insti-tuto

Tecnológico de Costa Rica (ITCR) has gained "Intel Associate" status and several new degree programmes. And Intel's presence has increased awareness of career opportunities in engineering and other technical fields. At the ITCR enrolment in engineering grew from 9.5% of students in 1997 to 12.5% in 2000.

Today the country is following a strategy that appears to enjoy strong support from key stakeholders: recognizing the need to liberalize telecommunications, improving infrastructure through private sector participation, improving the protection of intellectual property rights and improving access to foreign markets through free trade agreements with such countries as Canada, Chile and Mexico. Some reforms have met with resistance and open expressions of disagreement - all part of the policy debate in a pluralistic society.

After the US long-distance monopoly provider AT&T was broken up in 1984, the rates for long-distance telephone calls fell by 40%. In the midst of the Asian crisis the Korean mobile telephony market saw the number of subscribers double each year in 1996 -98 despite falling consumer demand. The entry of five competitive providers into the market, offering easy credit and subsidies for handsets. In Sri Lanka too, competition has led to more investment, more connectivity and better quality service. Internet service provision is competitive in the majority of countries surveyed in a recent study. But despite the benefits from competitive telecommunications markets, monopolies and duopolies continue to dominate for leased telephone lines and for local and long-distance telephony. And much remains to be done in such newer markets as paging, cable television and digital cellular telephony.

In many countries private monopolies have replaced state monopolies. And while many countries have privatized telecommunications quickly, they have built up regulatory capacity much more slowly. The nature and scope of regulatory reform greatly affect performance in telecommunications. For example, by pursuing regulation and privatization simultaneously, Chile has done much better than the Philippines, which put in place a regulatory system at a later stage.

Governments have a responsibility to promote research and development (R&D). Some R&D needs to be undertaken by the public sector, especially for people's needs that may not be met through the market. But governments are not responsible for doing all the R&D -and they can create incentives for other actors. Two mechanisms have been particularly important in promoting technology-oriented research -links between universities and industry, and fiscal incentives to promote R&D by private firms. Encouraging links between universities and industry can stimulate innovation.

High-technology companies thrive on state-of-the-art knowledge and creativity as well as the scientific and technical expertise of universities. Hubs are created as entrepreneurs purposely establish their businesses near universities. Tampere University of Technology in Finland links Nokia, the Technical Research Centre of Finland and firms in the wood processing industry. Industrialists in science and technology spend 20% of their time at universities, giving lectures to students in their areas of expertise. The "adjunct professors" work on a challenging interface between industry and academia, and students learn the relevance of technology to industry.

In China too, institutions of higher education support the technological work of enterprises. Tsinghua University established the Chemical Engineering and Applied Chemistry Institute jointly with Sino Petrochemical Engineering Company, which has given more than $3.6 million to support the university's research activities and recruited more than 100 of its graduates.

The State Torch Programme encourages enterprises to strengthen their ties with research institutions, to accelerate the commercialization of research results. Chinese universities have also established science parks. The Shanghai Technology Park acts as an incubator for the rapid application of scientific and technological work in industry.

In the 1990s China emphasized the development of high-technology industry through a variety of government programmes to support R&D. Now China is also using R&D to improve the productivity of traditional activities in agriculture. The Spark Programme propagates technologies to the countryside and assists farmers in using them for agricultural development.

Governments use a range of policy options to stimulate enterprise R&D. One is to provide matching funds for R&D. The Malaysian government contributes matching funds equivalent to 125% of the resources committed by private firms. Another is to co-finance R&D through a technology fund. Such funds allocate resources as a conditional loan, to be repaid if ventures succeed and written off otherwise.

Beyond promoting R&D, strong ties between industry and academia can also stimulate entrepreneurship. The Centre for Innovation and Entrepreneurship, an autonomous unit at Linköping University in Sweden, linked to the city's Foundation for Small Business Development, has applied technical know-how and financial resources to stimulate the growth and development of technology-based firms.

East Asian governments have used a variety of incentives to stimulate R&D by the private sector, drawing on a mix of public funding and tax breaks to encourage infirm R&D as well as collaboration among government agencies, universities and the private sector.

The Korean government has directly supported private R&D through incentives and other forms of assistance. It awarded firms tax-exempt funds for R&D activities (though the funds were subject to punitive taxes if not used within a specified period). The funds could also be invested in Korea's first venture capital fund, the Korea Technology Development Corporation, or in collaborative R&D efforts with public research institutes.

The government has given tax credits, allowed accelerated depreciation for investments in R&D facilities and cut taxes and import duties on research equipment. It has also used other tax incentives to promote technology imports. And the government has given grants and long-term, low-interest loans to companies participating in R&D projects and tax privileges and public funds to private and government R&D institutes.

But the main stimulus to industrial R&D in Korea came less from specific incentives than from the overall strategy-creating large conglomerates (chaebol), awarding them finance, protecting markets to allow them room to master complex technologies and then forcing them into export markets by removing protective barriers.

Korea's strategy for promoting technology has given the chaebol a strong base for entering into demanding mass production. While many aspects of the chaebol system fostered inefficiencies and are being reformed, Korea is nonetheless one of the most dramatic examples of rapid technological transformation.

As in Korea, the main impetus for rising R&D in Taiwan (province of China) came from an export orientation combined with measures to guide enterprises into more complex activities and reduce their dependence on technology imports. But the Taiwanese government did not promote the growth of large private conglomerates.

While the "lighter" industrial structure in Taiwan (province of China) meant less growth in private sector R&D compared with that in Korea, it was also a source of strength -leading to innovative capabilities that are more flexible, more responsive to markets and much more broadly spread in the economy.

The government started to support local R&D capabilities in the late 1950s, when a growing trade dependence reinforced the need to upgrade and diversify exports. A science and technology programme, started in 1979, targeted energy, production automation, information science and materials science technologies for development.

In 1982 biotechnology, electro-optics, hepatitis control and food technology were added to this list. A science and technology development plan for 1986-95 continued strategic targeting, aiming for R&D totalling 2 percent of GDP by 1995.

Around half the R&D is financed by the government. But enterprise R&D has risen as some local firms have expanded to become significant multinationals. The government has used a variety of incentives to encourage such R&D over the years, including providing venture capital and financing for enterprises that develop strategic industrial products.

The tax system provides full tax deductibility for R&D expenses, accelerated depreciation for research equipment and special incentives for enterprises based in the Hsinchu Science Park. The government also requires large firms to invest 0.5 -1.5 percent of their sales in R&D and has launched large-scale research consortiums, co-funded by industry, to develop critical products such as new-generation automobile engines and more sophisticated computer memory chips.

The Singapore government launched a $1.1 billion, five-year technology plan in 1991 to promote development in such sectors as biotechnology, microelectronics, information technology, electronic systems, materials technology and medical sciences. The plan set a target for R&D spending of 2% of GDP by 1995. A new plan, launched in 1997, doubled expenditure for science and technology, directing the funds to strategic industries to ensure future competitiveness.

Singapore uses several schemes to promote R&D by the private sector. The Cooperative Research Programme gives local enterprises grants (with at least 30% local equity) to develop their technological capabilities through work with universities and research institutions. The Research Incentive Scheme for Companies gives grants to set up centres of excellence in strategic technologies, open to all companies.

The R&D Assistance Scheme gives grants for specific product and process research that promotes enterprise competitiveness. And the National Science and Technology Board initiates research consortiums to allow companies and research institutes to pool their resources for R&D. Together these schemes have raised the share of private R&D to 65% of the total.

In 1986 Israel had only two venture capital funds, with less than $30 million in total investable assets. Today about 150 venture capital firms manage up to $5 billion in venture capital and private equity. The market took off in the early 1990s when the government set up a venture capital company, Yozma, to act as a catalyst for the emerging industry. With a budget of $100 million, Yozma invested in local companies and attracted foreign capital from Europe and the United States.

The Yozma fund is a model for the state-led emergence of a venture capital and high-technology industry. In India annual venture capital investments reached $350 million in 1998, with most concentrated in the technology hubs in the country's south and west. The government has developed policy guidelines to encourage venture capital, and the National Association of Software and Service Companies projects that up to $10 billion of venture capital may be available by 2008. In both India and Israel the government played an important role in establishing the venture capital industry and stimulating innovation, but a sophisticated financial sector was a precondition for attracting venture capital. Also key were strong ties to entrepreneurs and venture capitalists in the United States, and education systems that produce a significant number of highly skilled people, generating a critical mass for innovative activity.

Challenges of the Network Age

Today's technological transformations increase the premium on such skills and change the demand for different types of skills. This calls for a rethinking of education and training policies. In some countries systems need an overhaul. In others, a redirection of public funds. Greater resources and higher enrolments alone are not enough. The quality and orientation of education at each level, and the link with the demand for skills, are critical for mastering technology.

Primary education for all is essential. It develops some of the most basic capabilities for human development. And it creates a base of numeracy and literacy that enables people to be more innovative and productive. Although most countries in the low human development category have net primary enrolment ratios below 60%, most other developing countries have achieved nearly universal primary enrolment.

Secondary and higher education are also crucial for technology development. University education creates highly skilled individuals who reap the benefits through higher salaries. But it is also at the heart of creating national capacity to innovate, to adapt technology to the country's needs and to manage the risks of technological change-benefits that touch all of society.

In 1995 gross enrolment ratios averaged just 54% at the secondary level and 9% at the tertiary level in developing countries, compared with 107% and 60% in high-income OECD countries. Increasing the quantity of education is not enough, for it is the low quality of secondary schools that leads to low completion rates in many countries -and then low university enrolments.

Korea and Singapore built high university enrolments on high secondary completion rates in good schools. In internationally comparable tests in mathematics, students in Singapore, Korea, Japan and Hong Kong show the highest achievements. South Africa and Colombia, by contrast, performed significantly lower than the international average. Some differences across countries reflect differences in incomes.

But that is not the whole story. Korea ranks higher in test scores than countries with twice the GDP per capita, such as Norway. International comparisons, despite their problems, have two important advantages. First, they move the debate towards an assessment of outcomes rather than inputs, such as education budgets. Second, they force policy-makers to seek more refined measures to capture the quality of skills. Several countries, for example, have established national and local standards for assessing outcomes. These may not be internationally comparable, but they set important benchmarks. Assessments based on these standards make it clear that at the primary and secondary levels developing countries need to increase instruction time in science and mathematics, critical in improving students 'achievement in these subjects.

Chile is taking important strides to improve the quality of education, measuring the quality of outcomes and providing resources and incentives. And East Asia has shown that the technology orientation and content of education are as important as the expansion of resources.

In advanced economies education reform has placed new emphasis on helping people adapt to the new skill demands that come with shifting employment patterns. Students are encouraged to keep their education and career options open. In Denmark general courses in vocational programmes have opened new pathways to higher education. In the United Kingdom examination systems allow students to choose subjects from both general and vocational programmes.

In Finland the government has raised the status of vocational education and increased public resources for on-the-job learning. Since 1999 all three-year vocational courses have had to offer six months 'work experience to every student.

Using Technology to Improve Quality

With the rapid development of information and communications technology, it has become critical to teach basic computer skills to children. The biggest concern for developing countries is the lack of resources - both physical and human -to ensure adequate equipment and efficient teaching of such skills in schools. A computer costs more than the annual income of most people in developing countries, and teachers need to be trained to use new instructional material.

Yet information and communications technology also provides new possibilities for improving the quality of education at low cost. And there has been a proliferation of imaginative attempts in developing countries to spread new technology to education institutions in cost-effective ways.

Costa Rica launched a "computers in education "programme in 1998, aimed at raising the quality of education in primary schools. The programme uses an imaginative pedagogical approach to encourage interaction among children and raise cognitive skills.

The goal is to help transform education through changes in learning and teaching brought about by the use of computers, the training of teachers and the excitement generated by children's self-directed learning, knowledge creation and problem solving. The programme was designed to reach one- third of the country's primary school children, providing some 80 minutes of access to computers each week. Teacher surveys confirm that student performance has improved.

Chile is making a concerted effort to improve the quality of education. The key measures mark a shift in its education policies from a focus on inputs to a concern with outcomes:

- *National evaluation: A* comprehensive standardized testing system -Sistema de Medición de la Calidad de la Educación (SIMCE)- assesses Spanish and mathematics skills every two years for students in grades 4 and 8 and monitors schools' progress in improving outcomes.
- *Positive discrimination: A* government programme known as the P900 Programme targets assistance - from new textbooks and materials to professional support for teachers-to the 900 poorest primary schools.
- *Rewards: A* national system of performance evaluation for government-funded schools -Sistema Nacional de Evaluación del Desempeño de los Establecimientos Educacionales Subvencionados (SNED)- provides bonuses to all teachers in a school on the basis of student outcomes.

Made widely available and published in national newspapers, the SIMCE testing results have several uses:

— Policy-makers use the results to compare school performance nationally and identify schools needing special help.

— Schools use good results to market themselves and attract more students.

Parents use the results to help them select the best school for their children. SIMCE data are also used to assess the pace of progress among children attending the schools in the P900 Programme. Schools improving their results enough to "graduate" become part of the mainstream reform efforts for primary school and are replaced in the programme by other schools.

SNED has established competition between schools roughly comparable in student population and socioeconomic levels. Around 31,000 teachers received bonuses in each of the first two rounds of SNED awards.

Many parents, teachers and school administrators believe that this system of external standards and evaluation provides a good yardstick for measuring schools 'performance. Others think that SIMCE is unfair, especially to schools and students in poor neighbourhoods. Despite the controversy, Chile is clearly moving towards a more quality-oriented education system.

In Brazil a community schools programme is equipping young people in poor communities to use computers. The Committee for Democracy in Information Technology (CDI), a non-profit organization, is helping communities develop self-sufficient "information technology and citizenship schools". Communities that want to start a school must go through a rigorous process to ensure that they can sustain the school once CDI assistance ends. CDI provides free technical assistance for three to six months, trains the instructors, works with the school to procure an initial donation of hardware and then helps the school install the computers.

CDI has adapted its method to reach such diverse communities as street children and indigenous groups. As a result of its work in partnership with community associations, more than 35,000 children and young people, in 208 schools in 30 cities, have been trained in basic computer literacy.

Most schools charge the students a symbolic fee of $4 a month, equivalent to the cost of five roundtrip metro rides in Rio de Janeiro, to ensure their commitment. An interesting approach to improving Internet access and use relies on school networking initiatives, or "schoolnets". A few developing countries have established broad Internet access for schools through nationwide networks, among them Chile, Thailand and South Africa.

The Enlaces project in Chile has linked 5,000 basic and secondary schools to its network. Schools receive equipment, training, educational software and ongoing support from a technical assistance network of 35 Chilean universities organized by the Ministry of Education.

The aim is to connect all secondary schools and half the basic education institutions. The Enlaces network provides access to email and educational resources through the public telephone network, taking advantage of low overnight call charges. And La Plaza, a customized software interface developed locally, provides a virtual "meeting place" for teachers and students.

Over the past four decades the East Asian "tigers"- Hong Kong, Republic of Korea, Singapore and Taiwan (province of China)-achieved rapid development of human skills, equipping them for rapid progress in adapting technologies. Their success suggests strategies that less developed countries could consider and adapt to their own circumstances. One key lesson: the orientation and content of education are as important as resource allocation.

These countries not only invested in basic education but also emphasized a technology-oriented curriculum at higher levels. These investments in skills were part of an export-led development strategy, which provided demand signals for the skills required for improving competitiveness. Public education spending had been fairly low in East Asia, around 2.5% of GNP in 1960 for most countries. In 1997 the regional average was still only 2.9%, far less than the 3.9% average for all developing countries and the 5.1% average for Sub-Saharan African. But as the region's countries grew rapidly, so did the absolute level of spending on education. And education spending has also expanded as a share of national income, partly through increased private spending.

At an early stage of development East Asia gave priority to basic education, achieving universal primary schooling in the late 1970s. That made it easier to concentrate on improving quality and increasing resources in upper secondary and tertiary education. At the tertiary level enrolment ratios remained below 10% until 1975, contrasting unfavourably with those in Latin America. But as countries advanced, they needed more skilled and educated workers -and higher education expanded rapidly, especially after 1980. In Korea the tertiary enrolment ratio soared from 16% in 1980 to 39% in 1990 and then to 68% in 1996.

East Asia has taken a unique approach to financing education, relying on private sources for a relatively large share of spending, especially at the upper secondary and tertiary levels. And some countries have depended largely on the private sector to provide higher education. In Korea in 1993 private institutions accounted for 61% of enrolments in upper secondary education and 81% in tertiary education.

A large private role in providing education raises important questions about equity in access. Countries have used different approaches to address this issue. Korea targets public resources to basic education and is more selective about the mix of private and public resources at higher levels.

Singapore maintains relatively strong government involvement in the operation and financing of education at all levels. Evidence shows that privately financed institutions have lower unit operating costs. Not all developing countries can rely on private funding, but combining private and public funding at higher levels of education with public spending for primary and lower secondary levels is an option -as long as adequate access to higher education is assured for poor children. Here, grants, loans and subsidies can play a useful role.

East Asian governments opted for a strategy in which highly qualified, well-paid teachers work with more students. In Korea in 1975 pupil-teacher ratios exceeded 55 at the primary level and 35 at the secondary level, compared with developing country averages of 36 and 22. But Korea also pays teachers starting and mid-career salaries that are higher relative to per capita GNP than those in any other OECD country.

Continuous training was considered a key to developing human skills in the context of rapid technological change. As East Asian countries became more sophisticated, pressures emerged for governments and firms to provide effective education and training systems. In Korea, following enactment of the Vocational Training Law in 1967, the government established well-equipped public vocational training institutes and subsidized in-plant training programmes.

In the 1950s, when the government was seeking to develop the heavy and chemical industries, it promoted vocational high schools and junior technical colleges to satisfy the rising demand for technicians.

The government also established public education and research institutions to supply high-quality scientists and engineers, such as the Korea Institute of Science and Technology in 1967 and the Korea Advanced Institute of Science and Technology in 1971.

The government of Singapore took similar initiatives, launching a series of training programmes - Basic Education for Skill Training in 1983, Modular Skills Training in 1987 and Core Skills for Effectiveness and Changes in 1980. In the 1990s the government also led the development of the information and communications technology industry by supporting study in this area in tertiary institutions and building specialized training institutes as well as joint-venture institutes with private companies.

Thailand has developed the first nationwide, free-access network for education in South-East Asia. With only 120 dial-in telephone lines, the network was obliged to establish a system to optimize the use of the lines: it gave each school one account for Web browsing and no more than two for Web development, limiting total access to 40 hours a month. It also created a Website to increase schools 'awareness of the network and make Thai content available on the Internet.

The South African School Net (School-NetSA) is an interesting example for its structure and partnerships. SchoolNetSA, which is spread across several provinces, provides Internet services to local schools: connectivity, domain administration, email and technical support.

SchoolNetSA has also developed on-line educational content, and many schools have developed their own Web pages. Technologies such as CD-ROM, radio and cable television -or a mix of technologies -can be combined with the Internet to extend its reach.

The Kothmale Community Radio in Sri Lanka uses radio as a gateway to the Internet for its listeners in remote rural communities. Children or their teachers send requests for information about school topics for which no local resources exist; other listeners may also submit requests.

The broadcasters search for the information on the Internet, download it and make it available by constructing a broadcast around the information, mailing it to the school or placing it in the radio station 's open-access resource centre. The resource centre provides free Internet access and a library with computer databases, CD-ROMs, downloaded literature and print materials. This mediated access brings the Internet 's resources to rural and underserved communities. And community re-broadcasting can relay the information in local languages rather than English, the dominant language of the Internet.

Regional and global cooperation can reduce the cost of access to the Internet. Indeed, the development of information and communications technology provides the tools for learning through a global network. And wireless technologies enable developing countries with little telecommunications infrastructure to connect to the network.

A pan-African satellite system, to be launched later in 2001, is expected to provide cheaper and better network service to African countries. Satellite-based distance education systems can provide poor nations access to higher-quality education and training in advanced countries. Such initiatives can be part of cost-effective solutions for bridging the "digital divide "between countries.

Many universities in developing countries are testing or implementing Web-based education systems. The University of Botswana evaluated two distance education methods: an Internet-based course, free of charge, that ran three months, and a video-based course that ran one week. The Internet course boosted test results by 49% and the video technology by a similar amount, suggesting to the evaluators that both technologies have potential for distance learning.

The Indira Gandhi National University, established in 1985, has extended its communications capabilities to impart lifelong education and training, particularly to those living in rural and remote areas. Its sophisticated media centre has a satellite-based communications system, and all its education centres are equipped with computers and email access. Its Website provides general information and course material for all programmes.

The Internet is serving a growing number of learners, though it is still only a small part of a system using a wide range of communications technologies, including radio, television, cable television and teleconferencing. Other communities have developed the concept of the "virtual university ",using the Internet as a place for students, teachers and researchers to "meet ".

Working with universities in developing countries, the Francophone Virtual University supports distance education through advice, assistance and educational materials. A first call for proposals in 1998 resulted in the funding of 26 projects, mostly based on the Internet, and 132 more proposals from 16 countries are under consideration.

Formal education is only part of the skill creation system. Vocational and on-the-job training are just as important. When technology is changing, enterprises have to invest in worker training to remain competitive. They are more likely to do so when their workers are better educated to start with, since that lowers the cost of acquiring new skills.

Several studies -in Colombia, Indonesia, Malaysia and Mexico -have shown the high impact of enterprise training on firm productivity. Such training can be an effective and economical way to develop the skills of a workforce, particularly where employers are well informed about the skills needed. Some may also have the expertise and resources to provide training in both traditional and emerging skills.

The costs of enterprise training tend to be low compared with those of formal training, though employers lose part of the benefit if employees leave. Studies suggest that enterprise-based training yields higher private returns than other post-school training, in both developing and industrial countries. Enterprise training is also an essential complement to new investment in technology, plants and equipment.

Many studies in industrial countries suggest that the shortage of appropriate worker skills is a major constraint to the adoption of new technologies, while well-trained workers accelerate their adoption. Despite the demonstrated gains in productivity from training, not all employers provide it. Training involves costs -in materials, time and forgone production.

In Colombia, Indonesia, Malaysia and Mexico a sizable share of enterprises provide no worker training. Among small and medium-size enterprises, more than half provide no formal, structured training, and more than a third no informal training. Weak management, high training costs, inability to exploit scale economies in training, poor information about the benefits of training, market imperfections and the absence of competitive pressures -all are reasons that firms provide too little training.

Skill development requires policy intervention -in many forms. Governments can establish training centres that involve the private sector. Or they can use fiscal incentives or matching grants to encourage industry associations to establish and manage such centres. In East Asia industry associations provide many valuable training and technical services. Also worth considering are generous tax allowances to smaller firms for investing in training. And governments can sponsor coordination units to support interaction, with majority representation by the private sector to ensure that industry needs are addressed in the design of the training curriculum.

A comprehensive strategy for skill creation needs to address the entire range of market failures through a mix of institutional and other policies. Examples of such failures include a lack of information on education needs in industry and on student demands, inadequate incentives for trainers, low educational qualifications among employers and managers, low absorptive capacity among poorly educated workers and an inability to form efficient training programmes in line with changing skill and technology needs. Consider Singapore 's public funding and incentives for lifelong skill development, which try to overcome market deficiencies.

International benchmarking can be used to assess skill needs. And there may be a case for targeted development of new skills likely to be critical for future competitiveness, in such areas as food processing, capital-intensive process industries and electrical and electronics engineering. Such exercises can be undertaken by industry associations, academic institutions and government, working together.

Target special information and incentive programmes to small and medium-size enterprises to encourage them to invest in training. Governments can build on apprenticeship systems, in which craftspeople teach young workers traditional methods, upgrading the systems by setting up training centres and subsidizing · training by small and medium-size enterprises.

Provide recent secondary school graduates with partially financed training in accredited private centres, both encouraging skill acquisition and helping to create a market for private training. While most of these examples relate to training in the urban, industrial and service sectors, similar lessons apply in agriculture, where extension workers, researchers and others involved in technological upgrading also need training.

The Singapore government has invested heavily in developing high-level skills. It expanded the country 's university system and directed it towards the needs of its industrial policy, changing the specialization from social studies to technology and science.

In the process the government exercised tight control over the content and quality of curriculum, ensuring its relevance for the industrial activities being promoted. The government also devoted considerable efforts to developing the industrial training system, now considered one of the world 's best for high-technology production.

The Skill Development Fund, established in 1979, collected a levy of 1 percent of payroll from employers to subsidize training for low-paid workers. Singapore 's four polytechnics, which meet the need for mid-level technical and managerial skills, work closely with business in designing courses and providing practical training.

In addition, with government assistance under the Industry-Based Training Programme, employers conduct training courses matched to their needs. And the Economic Development Board continuously assesses emerging skill needs in consultation with leading enterprises and mounts specialized courses.

National investment in training reached 3.6 percent of annual payroll in 1995, and the government plans to raise it to 4 percent. Compare this with an average of 1.8 percent in the United Kingdom.

The programme 's initial impact was felt mostly in large firms. But efforts to increase small firms 'awareness of the training courses and to support industry associations have increased the impact on smaller organizations. To expand the benefit, a development consultancy scheme has been introduced to provide small and medium-size enterprises with grants for short-term consultancies in management, technical know-how, business development and staff training.

The social benefits of primary education -such as lower fertility and improved health for mothers and children -have made universal primary education a worldwide goal. But developing countries cannot ignore secondary and post-secondary education, though the social benefits from investments at these levels are less well documented.

The share of national income spent on education relative to, say, defence and health, is only a start. This indicator needs to be supplemented with others, such as teachers 'salaries relative to average incomes. Countries differ enormously in what they pay teachers.

In Uruguay, for example, the statutory salary of an experienced teacher at a public lower secondary school is just 80%($7,458 PPP US$) of average income. In Jordan a teacher with the same experience would earn almost 3.5 times ($11,594 PPP US$) the country 's average income. Offering starting salaries that are around the average income, or even lower, makes it difficult to attract enough qualified teachers.

An important indicator for higher education is the rate of enrolment in technical subjects such as science, engineering, mathematics and computing. Some developing countries have had great success in raising such enrolments. For example, of the 3 million students enrolled in college in the four East Asian "tigers "-Hong

Kong, Republic of Korea, Singapore and Taiwan (province of China)-in 1995, more than 1 million were in technical fields. China and India both have more than a million students enrolled in technical subjects. These large enrolments generate a critical mass of skilled personnel.

Tertiary education is expensive -too expensive for many poor countries. That leads to some difficult policy questions. The logic of government financing for secondary education is indisputable. Nor can governments neglect the post-secondary level. But public financing does need to be targeted to science, public health, agriculture and other fields in which technological innovation and adaptation will generate large spillover benefits for society as a whole.

For some developing countries, participating in regional and global networks of universities will make sense for several decades. But in the long run most will want to establish their own universities and research centres. Most developing countries already devote substantial public resources to education. But countries around the world find that they need to finance skill development through a mix of public resources, private finance and the direct contributions of individuals.

Financing education calls for a mix of public and private responsibility. The public sector must retain responsibility for universal primary education and for secondary and some tertiary education. But countries should consider allowing greater scope for private supply of some education services -and rely more on payments from individuals for advanced professional courses with strong market rewards.

Rich countries are opening their doors to developing country professionals -at a high cost to the home countries. About 100,000 Indian professionals a year are expected to take new visas recently issued by the United States. The cost of providing university educations to these professionals represents a resource loss for India of $2 billion a year.

This "brain drain "makes it more difficult for developing countries to retain the very people critical for technological development, people whose wages are increasingly set in the global marketplace.

India's Diaspora Network

The success of the Indian diaspora in Silicon Valley, for example, appears to be influencing how the world views India, by creating a sort of "branding ". Indian nationality for a software programmer sends a signal of quality just as a "made in Japan "label signals first-class consumer electronics. India 's information technology talent is now being courted not just by companies in the United States but by those in other countries.

The worldwide network of Indian professionals has been investing in skill development at home. The network has worked to raise the endowments and bolster the finances of some of India's institutions of higher education. And an effort is under way to establish five global institutes of science and technology.

The Indian diaspora is also having important effects in the information technology sector. Firms increasingly have operations in both the United States -the "front office "-and India -the "manufacturing facility".

At a time that talent in information technology has been scarce, Indian-launched firms in the United States have had a competitive advantage stemming from an unusual factor: they are up and running faster than their rivals simply because they can hire technical people faster, drawing as they do from a large transnational network.

This has led to rapidly growing demand for information technology specialists from India and thus to a rapid expansion of information technology training, increasingly by the private sector.

Korea and Taiwan (province of China) have focused more on encouraging their diasporas to return than on encouraging them to invest at home. Taiwan (province of China) set up a government agency -the National Youth Commission -to coordinate efforts to encourage return.

The commission acts as an information clearinghouse for returning scholars seeking employment and for potential employers. Korea has focused on upgrading its research institutions, such as the Korea Institute for Science and Technology (KIST), as a way to attract returnees. Those who join KIST are given a great deal of research and managerial autonomy. Both Korea and Taiwan (province of China) have tried hard to attract scholars and researchers.

Intensive recruiting programmes search out older professionals and scholars and offer them salaries competitive with overseas incomes, better working conditions and help with housing and children's schooling. Visiting professor programmes allow the countries to tap the expertise of those uncertain about returning home for good. In the 1960s just 16% of Korean scientists and engineers with doctorates from the United States returned to Korea. In the 1980s that share jumped about two-thirds. A large part of the difference was due to Korea's improved economic prospects.

Today, rather than focusing only on the physical return of their pools of technological talent living abroad, the two countries are working to plug their diasporas into cross-national networks. They are organizing networks of professionals overseas and linking them with the source country.

Many African countries have suffered from internal conflicts and stagnant economies. Many skilled people have left this hostile environment. The Return of Qualified African Nationals Programme, run by the International Organization for Migration, has tried to encourage qualified nationals to return and helped them reintegrate. It reintegrated 1,857 nationals in 1983-99, slightly more than 100 a year. Given the high level of brain drain from Africa, this effort is unlikely to make much of a difference.

A diaspora's expertise and resources can be invaluable, but effectiveness depends on the state of affairs in the home country. That means that it must have an environment conducive to economic development, with political stability and sound economic policies.

The diaspora's attitude towards returning to the home country is likely to change as the country develops and its prospects improve. Both the Indian and Korean diasporas responded to improving domestic conditions. Timing and chance play a part in this, but in the end diaspora networks can be effective only when countries get their houses in order.

5

E-Services

The increasing demand for Information and communications technologies (ICT) has generated major growth in communication services, which are expanding in all countries. Through e-commerce, the services industries have enjoyed an increase particularly in cross-border trade. The digitization of business processes, coupled with the universality of the Internet, has allowed companies to outsource activities and services to more cost-effective locations as well as to access new clients in foreign markets.

As a result of these changes in the global services market, an increasing number of countries, including developing ones, are directing their efforts towards expanding their services exports. Their objective is to increase export capacities in services that are increasingly in demand on the global market, and to become more competitive in exporting these services.

The role of manufactured goods exports in enhancing a country's global competitiveness has been widely acknowledged. Using trade flow analysis as a standard approach for assessing competitiveness, these studies have found that countries which have succeeded in gaining market share over a sustained time period are also gaining competitive advantage. By contrast, few studies have examined exports of commercial services as indicators of increasing competitiveness, despite the fact that services trade accounts for 20 per cent of total world trade and has grown as rapidly as merchandise trade (8.5%) over the past 15 years. In particular, the increasing use of ICT in the services sector has played an important role in enhancing international trade in services.

Studies on the impact of ICT and e-commerce on productivity growth in the United States have shown that labour productivity growth in the services sectors (measured by value added per full-time employee) has been particularly high in sectors such as wholesale and retail trade and financial and personal services. Other studies based on macroeconomic or computable general equilibrium (CGE) models have supported the argument that e-commerce has a positive impact on productivity and growth.

Knowledge- and information-based services, such as communications, computer, financial, insurance and royalty services, are contributing an increasing share of GDP in many OECD countries. In Canada, the value added of telecommunications services increased by 19 per cent from 1998 to 1999, accounting for 2.5 per cent of total GDP, up from 1.9 per cent in 1990. In the Republic of Korea, the share of the IT industry (20 per cent of which is based on IT services) in GDP increased from 8.6 per cent (1997) to 13 per cent (2000). In the Philippines, the share of communication services (combined with transportation and storage) in GDP increased by 4.6 per cent from 1999 to 2000, to 9.9 per cent, largely due to the growing use of cellular phones and the increasing accessibility of Internet and cable services.

Traditionally, the competitiveness of a country has been identified with the performance of its exports. A country's firms and industries are considered competitive in products in which they are increasing world market share. Furthermore, countries that provide a favourable environment for companies to operate in, which allows them to develop innovations and exploit new market opportunities, also tend to be successful exporters. The dynamism and performance of exports often explain the conditions under which firms operate and the difficulties they face. As most firms are price takers in international markets, gaining market share over a sustained period of time usually requires the achievement of competitive advantage. In this sense, export performance is a good indicator of competitiveness.

Export performance can be measured in a number of ways. The 2 most common approaches and indicators for measuring export competitiveness are:

- The revealed comparative advantage (RCA) index, which measures relative export performance by country and industry or product, defined as a country's share of world exports of a good divided by its share of total world trade; and
- Dynamism of demand, measured by changes in the world market shares (WMS) of a given product over a certain period of time; the rate of growth over alternative periods; and the rate of growth in a product's share in world exports.

Services activities contribute a major share to national output. For example, services value added contributed 71 per cent to Europe's GDP in 1999 and 67 per cent to Canada's. While these figures are globally the highest, it can safely be said that the share of services value added increased between 1990 and 1999 in all regions. In 1999, it comprised 62 per cent of GDP in Latin America, 41 per cent in East Asia and 56 per cent in Sub-Saharan Africa. Hence, services activities are an increasingly important sector for economic development and growth.

At the same time, exports of services are becoming increasingly important. Between 1990 and 2000, world trade in services grew at an annual average rate of 6.6 per cent, which almost equals the rate for merchandise trade (6.8%). Growth rates in developing countries' services exports were particularly high, accounting for 10.1 per cent over the 10-year period, compared to 9.5 per cent annual growth in merchandise trade exports. The share of services in world exports amounted to 19.6 per cent in 1999. Developing countries also account for a growing share of world trade in services. While in 1990 their share in world exports amounted to 15.7 per cent, it had increased to 21.2 per cent by 2000. Over the same period, their share in world imports increased from 20 per cent (1990) to 22.7 per cent (2000).

On the export side, in 2000, developed countries accounted for 79 per cent of world exports in services and 72 per cent of exports in goods. However, their share in both goods and services exports is shrinking as developing countries are gaining international market share. The services exports of the latter grew at an annual average rate of more than 10 per cent between 1990 and 2000, and their merchandise exports at a rate of 9.5 per cent. Developed countries' exports, on the other hand, grew by only 5.9 per cent (merchandise exports) and 5.4 per cent (services exports) during the same period.

As far as imports are concerned, the developing countries' share in the world market is similar to their export share, 27 per cent in merchandise imports and 23.6 per cent in services imports. However, the developing countries' share has not increased as much in imports as in exports over the 10-year period; their annual growth rates for services imports are 7.9 per cent (compared to 10 per cent for exports) and for merchandise imports 8.7 per cent (compared to 9.5% for exports). Based on this, we can conclude that developing countries' services exports account for the most dynamic changes in world trade in the past 10 years.

The main exporter of services is the United States, which accounted for 20 per cent of the global market in 2000. It is followed by the United Kingdom, Germany, France and Japan, which combined account for almost half of all services exports. Among the developing countries, major services exporters are Hong Kong (China), China, the Republic of Korea, Singapore, Turkey and India. On the importing side, the United States, followed by Germany, Japan, the United Kingdom and France, dominate 44 per cent of the world market. The main developing country services importers are China, the Republic of Korea, Hong Kong (China), Saudi Arabia, Singapore and India. In fact, developing Asia accounts for almost two-thirds of all developing-country services exports, whereas Africa's share is minimal, partly due to the scant statistics available from the region.

Travel, transportation and other business services constitute by far the most important services exports and also reflect the main services exports in developed countries. In developing countries, travel takes the largest share of exports, followed by other business services and transport services. The traditional distribution of services exports in the developing countries have very small market shares in the newly emerging services such as royalties and license fees, computer and information services, and financial and insurance services. Whereas they take 23 per cent of the world market in travel services. An interesting exception is the 20 per cent market share of the developing countries in communication services exports, a fairly recent development.

Exports experiencing above-average growth over a certain time period are considered "dynamic". The following services can be considered to have been dynamic at the global level during the 10-year period:

— Computer-related services (31%)

— Personal, cultural and recreational services (20%)

— Communication services (15%)

— Financial services (10.6%)

— Royalties and license fees (10.4%)

— Construction services (8.8%).

At the five-year level, the same types of services can be identified as dynamic, with the exception of construction services, which experienced negative growth between 1995 and 2000. Overall, export growth slowed during the five-year period, with the exception of financial services exports, which grew at an annual rate of 13 per cent, compared to 10.6 per cent over the 10-year period.

A comparison of developing and developed countries' growth rates for different types of services exports reveals that the developing countries' services growth rates were higher than the world average for all of the dynamic services, and particularly high for three services: computer and information services (58%), personal, cultural and recreational services (53%) and financial services (41%). It is important to keep in mind, though, that the global market shares of developing countries in computer and financial services trade are still very low (less than 3% respectively). In order to account for high growth rates resulting from a low initial base, growth rates of shares in world services exports were considered.

As a result, all of the dynamic services saw their shares in world exports increase during the 10-year period, whereas all of the non-dynamic services (i.e. those with below-average value growth rates) saw their shares in the world export market decrease. Hence, the growth rates of shares confirm the dynamic services identified based on value growth rates. They also confirm that computer-related services are by far the most dynamic export service: this sector gained 23.3 per cent market share between 1990 and 2000.

Except for construction services, all of the dynamic services are ones that can easily be provided electronically. Hence one can safely conclude that, except for insurance services and other business services, all services that can be provided electronically - so-called "e-services" - are also dynamic export services. This supports the notion that e-commerce and ICT have an important role to play in changing the pattern of international trade in services.

Which countries have a comparative advantage in the export of e-services? Which countries are gaining ground in the international markets for dynamic services? To answer the first question, the following discussion will first present a calculation of the revealed comparative advantage (RCA) index. Then, to address the second question, it will look at changes in countries' world market shares (WMS) during the five-year period to identify which countries have improved their export competitiveness in dynamic e-services. The services categories focused on include communication, financial, computer, royalties and license fees and personal, cultural and recreational services.

An RCA of greater than one indicates a region's (country's) specialization or comparative advantage in exporting a particular service. Interestingly, developing countries (as a group) have a comparative advantage in exporting communication services, whereas developed countries have a comparative advantage in all the other selected services. This also reflects the rapid growth that communication services exports have experienced in the developing countries during the 10-year period (23%).

A closer look at the five-year period reveals that in both insurance services and personal, cultural and recreational services, developing countries have an index very close to one, and in some years their RCA was even greater than one. Hence, in these services they are close to gaining comparative advantage, whereas in others, such as computer-related services and royalties, they (as a group) have no comparative advantage.

Few developing countries have a comparative advantage in more than one sector. Exceptions include Mexico (communications and personal, cultural and recreational services), Panama (financial and computer services), Ecuador (communications and personal, cultural and recreational services, but a strong negative trend), and Costa Rica (communications and computer services).

While in most of the services categories the developed countries clearly dominate, the communications services category includes many developing countries. Developing countries' exports in communications services have grown strongly during the past decade and many developing countries have specialized in the export of this service.

Another case worthwhile mentioning is that of the Eastern European countries, including Bulgaria, the Czech Republic, Hungary, Latvia, Macedonia, Romania and Slovakia, all of which appear in this most dynamic and competitive group of services exporters. Finally, it should be noted that many developing countries, while not yet having a comparative advantage in exporting e-services, showed positive RCA growth rates during the five-year period, indicating that they are gaining comparative advantage. Some of them are likely to join the most dynamic group of e-services exporters within a few years.

While the RCA index provides information about a country's comparative advantage in exporting a certain product (and changes in the index indicate whether a country gained or lost comparative advantage), the calculation of WMS indices allows the identification of countries that have gained world market shares in the export of specific services during a certain time period.

Hence, while the RCA considers only the country's exports and its degree of specialization, the WMS places these exports in the context of the world market. An increase or decrease in WMS thus indicates whether a country is becoming more or less competitive at the global level.

A change in the WMS index as measured here does not reflect the actual percentage share of a country's export product in the world market, but only the factor by which this share has changed. In other words, a country with a very small share in world exports could have a positive or high average WMS index over the five-year period. The purpose of this exercise is not to show which countries are the main exporters but to identify those that gained market share and thus increased their competitiveness.

Most dynamic countries have been the most successful in increasing their WMS in the export of e-services and thus have become more competitive. They include many developing countries, which in particular account for 50 per cent of communications and financial services exports and about 40 per cent of royalty services exports. Also noteworthy is the dominance of the Eastern European countries, many of which have successfully increased their WMS in the export of e-services.

In communication services, both China and Morocco had rapid growth in their comparative advantage and market share indicators during the five years in question. In financial services, a small island nation - Saint Vincent and the Grenadines - succeeded in substantially increasing its competitiveness in the world market. Among computer and information services, Costa Rica is clearly the outstanding case and will be considered in more detail below. As far as royalty services exports are concerned, the case of Paraguay is special, since its indicators are largely based on the export of hydropower. In the area of personal and cultural services, Mexico has experienced the most dynamic growth in gaining competitiveness and market share.

Unlike these "rising stars", many countries fall in the middle range. They may be gaining competitiveness, characterized by positive growth of either their RCA or their WMS indices; or they may have a comparative advantage and high market share but negative trends (e.g. losing market share and competitiveness in the short to medium term). Finally, losses in market share in one product or service may be accompanied by gains in market share in other products; hence, each case needs to be interpreted individually.

Computer-related services play a key role in the development of knowledge-based services because they produce high-value-added services. Although the developed countries dominate the computer industry, some developing countries have been successful in tapping into the computer-related service market, providing software and IT-enabled services, and showing high export growth rates in these sectors. Besides their potential role in export-led growth, computer software and services also play an important economic role in facilitating growth and development in other domestic industries, which increasingly depend on software as a core component in their design, production and distribution processes.

Export-driven development strategy in Costa Rica

Costa Rica is well known for an export-driven development strategy based on the ICT sector. Exports grew exponentially during the 1990s, from $ 1.6 billion (1990) to $ 6.7 billion (1999), followed by a decrease in 2001/02. During the same period, there was a clear shift from traditional to non-traditional exports, largely based on the exports of IT-related products, which experienced annual growth rates of up to 500 per cent (1998). While "office and telecommunications equipment" accounted for only 0.1 per cent of exports in 1995, this share had increased to 41 per cent of exports by 1999. By 2001, one product category (computer parts/modular circuits) accounted for the largest share in exports (15.6%), followed by bananas (10%).

This development resulted largely from the establishment in Costa Rica of Intel, one of world's largest producers of electronic components. The success of the Costa Rican IT industry (and the ability of the country to attract foreign investment in this sector) can be explained by a number of factors, such as the country's geographic location, its political stability, its educated workforce and its advanced infrastructure, coupled with policies that improved the telecommunications infrastructure and services, attracted foreign investment and, generally, heavily promoted the country's assets abroad.

While the development and growth of the IT-producing industry in Costa Rica is well researched, little attention has been paid thus far to another fast-growing export sector of the Costa Rican economy: exports of computer- and information-related services.

The share of computer-related services exports in Costa Rica's total services exports has increased from almost 0 to 3.2 per cent in just three years. Computer-related services exports account for an important share of total exports and have overtaken sugar exports (their share is double that of sugar exports). What prompted this extraordinary development? One explanation can be found in the fact that the growth of the domestic IT industry and the favourable environment it brought about also led an increasing number of companies to use ICT in their business activities, moving rapidly into e-commerce, e-banking or e-tourism. In particular, the past decade saw the creation of a significant number of enterprises (small to large) offering computer-related (in particular software) services and products.

The computer-related service industry started to develop in Costa Rica in the 1980s, but really took off in the early 1990s. 30 per cent of the companies were created during the 1980s and 70 per cent during the 1990s, mainly with domestic capital. Over 80 per cent of the companies are locally owned and about half of them export their services. While initially most of the companies produced for the domestic market, beginning in 1999 they rapidly expanded into the international market.

So far, computer-related services have been dominated by software services. It has been estimated that software production has a national value added exceeding 90 per cent. The Costa Rican software production derives mainly from small and medium-sized enterprises producing tailor-made applications or providing advisory services in the area of software development for other companies.

A survey by Mata and Vartanián indicated that 88 per cent of the software companies offer tailor-made software services, 60 per cent software packages, 39 per cent software consulting and 22 per cent other services. The sector is characterized by rapid sales growth: between 1997 and 2000, 30 per cent of the companies doubled their sales. Even faster growth was predicted for the next few years: 55 per cent of the companies expect their sales to double between 2000 and 2003.

Initially, most software companies served the domestic market. As of 2000, half of the companies produced for export, but only 16 per cent (mainly the larger companies) exclusively served the export market. Only 9 per cent of the companies exported more than $1 million per year (28% exported between $100,000 and 500,000 and 53% less than $100,000).

Hence, the rapid export growth during the three-year period is likely to be based on exports by large companies. According to the survey, export growth rates accelerated between 1997 and 1999: 14 per cent of the companies increased their exports by more than 100 per cent, 26 per cent by more than 51 per cent and 45 per cent by more than 30 per cent.

The software sector is essentially a knowledge-based industry requiring highly skilled professionals, and a large pool of educated labour has allowed Costa Rican companies to successfully enter this sector. The government has played an important role in creating an educated population by continuously expanding the education system and including IT in the curriculum. This policy has been pursued actively by the government in its channelling of defence spending to education.

Costa Rica has a tradition of investing heavily in education and is currently spending 6 per cent of its GDP on education. The key factors influencing the development of the software sector are the availability of highly skilled employees, possibilities for training and capacity building, the number of IT professionals available and the legal framework in the country.

Acknowledging the sector's dynamism and growth potential, the Inter-American Development Bank (IDB) in 1999 approved a project to develop the software sector in

Costa Rica. The project aims to improve the sector's competitiveness in the global market as well as make local software companies engines of economic development by helping them produce hard-currency revenue and create high-paying jobs. The project emphasizes training and curriculum building for software technicians to improve the overall technical capabilities in the country and to enable local software producers to compete in the international market.

The project, which is ongoing, is carried out in cooperation with PROCOMER (Promotora del Comercio Exterior de Costa Rica), CAPROSOFT (Cámara de Productores de Software) and CENAT (Centro de Alta Tecnología), each of which contributes financially to the project and participate actively in it.

Given the small size of the domestic market, Costa Rican software companies aim at the export market. The advantages enjoyed by Costa Rica in comparison with other Latin American countries also developing their software sector include a pool of low-cost skilled . IT workers and current trade agreements in the North American market.

Nevertheless, software exporters face a number of challenges in their efforts to increase their software services and exports, such as growing competition in the global market, the unavailability of export financing and the lack of an existing structure to support their clients in the export market. The expensive air travel within the region, barriers faced in foreign markets, the lack of export marketing and distribution channels and the migration from proprietary systems to open platforms are further obstacles mentioned by software exporters .

Business processes outsourcing in India

The Indian software sector has been studied extensively because of its breathtaking growth during the past decade, Exports of software and related services have increased from less than $500 million (1994/95) to almost $8 billion (2001/02). Between 1999/00 and 2001/02, exports grew from $3.9 billion to $6.2 billion, an increase of almost 60 per cent. Software exports now comprise more than 16 per cent of India's total exports. A revised version of an often-cited NASSCOM-McKinsey study estimates that IT services exports will reach $77 billion by 2008, contributing 10 per cent to the country's GDP (up from 2% in 2002) and 30 per cent of all foreign exchange (up from 8%) and creating four million new (direct and indirect) jobs.

These figures comprise both software services and IT-enabled services- increasingly called business process outsourcing (BPO) - such as those related to customer interaction centers, back-office operations, revenue accounting, data entry and transcription services or GIS (geographic information system) services. Revenues are expected to reach $1.5 billion by the end of 2002. IT-enabled services exports grew at over 45 per cent annually in 1999 and 2000 and 70 per cent annually during 2001 and 2002. The number of jobs created by this sector is expected to increase from 107,000 (2001-02) to 1.1 million (2008), generating revenues of $21 - 24 billion.

Overshadowed by the exponentially growing software sector during the 1990s, BPO in India received little attention from researchers or the business community until the start of the new millennium. It has now become the new buzzword, reflecting this sector's great potential for creating new business opportunities and suggesting that the sector will grow quickly in the short to medium term.

BPO refers to outsourcing (often, but not necessarily, by big multinational companies) of business processes and functions in the areas of administration, finance, human resources, distribution logistics, manufacturing services, sales, marketing and customer care to locations that can provide these services at a lower cost through highspeed data communication links, which guarantee timely delivery of the data and services.

BPO often involves large-scale data processing (such as that required by banks, insurance companies and airlines) - for example, in revenue accounting and payroll processing. These IT-intensive outsourced tasks range from routine business processes to strategic tasks directly affecting revenues. As a result of the improved global telecommunications infrastructure, companies now have the choice to outsource their business processes to service providers located (almost) anywhere in the world. This allows management to focus on building core business activities and cut back spending on office facilities and computer systems.

While BPO is clearly a cost-driven process, the potential to continuously improve processes as well as service levels is an additional reason for out-sourcing. Projections for the BPO market are extremely high: it is expected to grow from less than $300 billion (2001) to close to $1 trillion by 2007. Today, distribution and logistics take the largest share of the market (29%), followed by human resources (24%) and payment services (16%). According to a survey by Forrester (2002) with 57 Global 3,500 firms, more than 50 per cent of the companies reported spending more than $1 million annually on BPO. Forrester predicts that the BPO market in the United States will increase annually by 70 per cent (2000-6). Even if these figures are exaggerated, there is undoubtedly huge business potential in the BPO market.

India is planning to capture a significant share of the BPO world market by 2007-08. However, the Indian BPO sector is still in its initial stages, often capturing outsourced overflow work from international BPO service providers rather than receiving direct contracts. Many of the large BPO providers are foreign affiliates working from India (such as GE, Dell or American Express) and staffed and managed by Indians. According to NASSCOM, the IT industry's national association, there are currently 204 Indian companies providing IT-enabled services. Most of them focus on financial, telecommunications and manufacturing services. The latest NASSCOM-McKinsey report cited earlier suggests that the banking and insurance sectors are likely to provide the greatest opportunities in offshore BPO, followed by the telecommunications, retail, utilities, automotive, computer and pharmaceuticals sectors.

India is building heavily on its already well-established software and IT-enabled service industries. The initial phase of IT-enabled services in India was dominated by customer contact centers (e.g. call centers) and transaction-intensive services (e.g. back-office operations and data processing, medical transcriptions, content development and administration). These services are considered to be lower in the value chain than more specialized services like research and development (R&D) or customized business services. Like the latter, BPO is viewed as being higher in the value chain, since it involves the complete management of a process.

Indian companies are planning to develop the quality of their BPO services by applying a new business framework created by Carnegie Mellon University (CMU) of the United States. This so-called eServices Capability Model (escm) employs best practices for measuring and improving the value of outsourcing relationships, such as increased productivity, reduced cycle time, decreased transaction costs and improved time to the market. CMU also provides certification of service providers' capabilities and performance, which assures clients of high quality and reduced risk when they do business with a certified provider.

Companies based in the United States or Europe increasingly look to India in their efforts to outsource part of their software development to more cost-effective locations. NASSCOM estimates that during the period 2000-2001, one in four of the global majors outsourced its key software development to India; they also report that 82 per cent of United States companies rank India as their first choice for software out-sourcing.

The reputation built over the past decade is one key reason why companies look to India for BPO. Other advantages include the large pool of English-speaking IT and engineering graduates, which the Government is augmenting by taking steps, such as establishing Indian Institutes of Technology in various cities, to triple the number of engineering students by 2008. Furthermore, India's time zone vis-à-vis the United States encourages BPO with the latter as it allows, for example, companies based on the United States East Coast to provide customer services 24 hours a day.

The potential for India to become a hub for IT-enabled services (particularly BPO) has been recognized by the Indian Government and NASSOM, both of which have started a dialogue aimed at defining and creating a favourable environment for each segment of the IT-enabled services sector. These efforts include actions in the areas of tax exemption, telecommunications infrastructure, financial assistance for start-ups, establishment of a venture capital (VC) fund, training and the promotion of entrepreneurship and teleworking for women in the IT-enabled sector.

Business based on outsourcing is highly dependent on the volatility of foreign markets. As Indian BPO exporters are largely focused on the United States market, a downturn in their main export market could negatively affect their business. For example, in the software sector (which is equally dependent on the United States market), the Nasdaq crash led to cuts in IT investment, which directly affected Indian programmers and led to an oversupply of IT professionals in India. Fortunately, IT-enabled services were less affected by the recession in the United States because they are the indispensable back-office processes of brick-and-mortar companies. By contrast, the slow-down of the United States economy has prompted an increasing number of companies to outsource to India to maintain their margins.

New market entrants such as China and the Philippines may pose serious competition to Indian BPO providers within a few years' time. In particular, if the BPO business model is based primarily on cost advantage and low labour cost, it can be easily replicated elsewhere, leading to a constant decrease in profit margins. Therefore, Indian companies have a great interest in working continuously to develop more sophisticated, specialized and higher-value-added BPO services to safeguard their current leadership position in the world market. This will require specialists not only in the IT and engineering professions but also in other areas such as medicine, law, accountancy, statistics and human resource management.

International telephony was deregulated on 1 April 2002, and since then prices have dropped significantly, favouring IT-enabled services such as call centres. However, to respond to the needs of the emerging BPO sector, deregulation should go further and allow interconnectivity between networks and different Internet service providers, the establishment of international gateways by the IT-enabling industry and deregulation of international bandwidth to allow companies to buy high-capacity cable and satellite connectivity at competitive prices.

6

Challenges of Internet Applications

The Internet is really a network of networks and is comprised of a number of different technologies and infrastructures. It provides immediate access to information from around the world. With simple e-mail, it is as easy to send a message to another continent as it is to the building next door. Through the World Wide Web, thousands of newspapers and tens of thousands of other information sources are available from around the world. While access is still not available to most of the world's population, the fastest rates of growth are in less developed countries.

Internet was designed by purpose to be decentralized, to work without gatekeepers, and to accommodate multiple, competitive access points. The absence of gatekeepers of the kind that exist in broadcasting, cable television, or satellite transmission, the availability of numerous hosting sites, and the irrelevance of geographic location mean that material can almost always be published outside the control of governments, monopolies or oligopolies.

The Internet has low barriers to access. Service can be priced very inexpensively. The costs of creating and disseminating content are extremely low. Because of the Internet, anybody who has a computer and a modem can be a publisher — a digital Gutenberg.

The digitization of information and the ability to transmit it over the telephone network, combined with the decentralized nature of the Internet, mean that the Internet has essentially unlimited capacity to hold information. In economic terms, the marginal cost of adding another web site, sending another email message, or posting to a newsgroup is essentially zero.

All Internet users can be both speakers and listeners. The net allows responsive communication from one-to-one, from one-to-many, and from many-to-one. Itallows users to exercise far more choice than even cable television or short wave radio. The user can skip from site to site in ways that are not dictated by the content providers or by the access provider. User can control what content reaches their computers. Users can encrypt their communications to hide them from government censors.

The Internet is not linked to any infrastructure other than the telephone system. Dial-up access is available from any telephone that can make an international call. Access to the Internet can also be wireless and satellite based and therefore further removed from effective control of governments.

In a 1996 Communication, the European Commission noted:

> "A unique characteristic of the Internet is that it functions simultaneously as a medium for publishing and for communication. Unlike in the case of

> traditional media, the Internet supports a variety of communication modes: one-to-one, one-to-many, many-to-many. An Internet user may "speak" or "listen" interchangeably. At any given time, a receiver can and does become content provider, of his own accord, or through "re-posting" of content by a third party. The Internet therefore is radically different from traditional broadcasting. It also differs radically from a traditional telecommunication service."

The European Commission Legal Advisory Board, which advises the European Commission on legal matters concerning the European information market, also recognized the uniqueness of the Internet, calling it "a positive instrument, empowering citizens and educators, lowering the barriers to the creation and distribution of content and offering universal access to ever richer sources of digital information."

The United States Supreme Court, in ruling that the Communications Decency Act was unconstitutional and that the Internet merited the strongest protection of free expression, based its judgment on the conclusion that the Internet was "a unique and wholly new medium of worldwide human communication." The vast new potential of the Internet for expanding access to information and participation in government and civil society has already begun to show itself with concrete contributions to democracy and human rights.

The bi-directional nature of the Internet has tremendous potential for fostering democratic participation, giving voice to the voiceless. The Internet could allow citizens to communicate with their government, to pose questions to their elected representatives, and to submit comments on pending issues. While many governments have been slow to take advantage of the democratic potential of the Internet, some harbingers of progress can be seen. In January 1995, the municipality of Bologna created the Iperbole system — a free-of-charge "civic network" offering citizens and businesses an opportunity to send requests, suggestions, claims and complaints by email to more than 1,300 municipal offices. The system also includes discussion and newsgroups dealing with specific topics, suggested by citizens, business enterprises, public and private institutions, and by the municipal administration itself. The UK conducted a one-time on-line consultation on the government's freedom of information proposal.

Western governments are not the only ones that have begun to respond. In Hungary earlier this year, Hungary's iNteRNeTTo held an online debate between politicians from the two leading parties. The Costa Rican government, to make voting more convenient, is working to shift to an electronic voting system. Taking advantage of a literacy rate of 94% and the fact that about 50% of grade schools have Internet-connected computers, Costa Rica hopes to run an entirely electronic balloting in 2002. International bodies also use the Internet to promote public participation in their activities. For example, last year the EU conducted an online forum regarding illegal or harmful content on the Internet. Grassroots organizations can use the Internet to mobilize voters to be active on issues. One example is the Adopt your Legislator campaign developed by CDT in the US.

One of the most important potential benefits of the Internet is the ability to provide rapid access to the full text of government documents. If a government is willing, it can provide its citizens access to enacted and proposed laws, regulations, government reports and statistics, transcripts of parliamentary debates, judicial decisions, all searchable by word or concept. Information previously available only to experts, usually only in the capital city, and often only with great expenditure of time and money can now be made available to individuals in the smallest rural town and at public libraries in the poorest neighborhoods. This vast openness need not be the luxury of only wealthy nations.

In almost every country in the world, most government information is now created by word processing, meaning that the information is already digitized. Again, if the government is willing, the information can be rapidly and inexpensively put on-line, even using simple Gopher technology. Many nations have begun to use the Internet, nations as diverse as the United Kingdom, the Czech Republic, and South Africa. The European Union is a most effective user of the Web to make its voluminous publications available to a wide audience. Some examples from the U.S. include THOMAS, the Website of the Library of Congress and GPO Access providing access to materials from the Government Printing Office, including all proposed federal regulations, and transcripts of daily Congressional debates.

The Internet has opened up new opportunities for discourse, on matters political, intellectual, and personal. The Internet's architecture allows for a diversity of views and exchange of information that is simply not possible in any other media. As of August 1998, one service identified 29,000 IRC (Internet Relay Chat) channels, 30,000 Usenet newsgroups, and 90,095 mailings lists — each one representing a network of individuals worldwide interested in a particular subject. The Web has become a place where there is ready access to newspapers and other publications. A wide range of print publications are available on-line, and many broadcast media now have on-line services that allow searching of past broadcasts, a capability previously available only to governments and a few research institutes. The Radio Free Europe/Radio Liberty Newsline illustrates the use of old-fashioned e-mail to disseminate information to a dispersed audience very inexpensively. The Internet makes it possible for more organizations to distribute news and commentary, increasing the diversity of voices. The Association for Independent Media in Bosnia has made use of the Internet, both e-mail and the World Wide Web. AIM operates on the principle of a mail-box system. Information is exchanged via a central computer located in Paris. AIM texts are available in Serbian, Croatian, Bosnian, and a choice of texts is available in English. Subscribers to AIM regularly receive the whole production of AIM via e-mail. The China News Digest makes available news from non-official sources. While the site is sometimes blocked by the Chinese government, users in China have found ways to access it. The service also uses e-mail to disseminate its news within China.

The Internet offers creative ways to disseminate information around the controls of censors. Radio B92 in Belgrade is one of the leading examples of this. When authorities shut down the radio station, it put its programming on the Internet through RealAudio, using a Dutch service provider; Radio Free Europe, Voice of America, and Deutche Welle picked up the station off the Net and rebroadcast it back into Serbia, where it served as the source of independent reporting and a focal point for democratic opposition. Faced with this strategy, the government allowed the station back on the air. In June of 1997, Chinese dissidents founded *Tunnel*, a Chinese language journal of dissent. Tunnel is managed and edited in China. Once an issue is ready to be published, it is secretly delivered to the United States and then emailed back to China from an anonymous address. "Thus its staff remains safely hidden in cyberspace, and all of its contributors, both in China and abroad, write under pseudonyms."

The technology of the Internet frustrates control in other ways. Proxy servers purportedly block access to web sites known to contain objectionable content and thus preclude such content from being accessed. Such servers fail to achieve their goal, however, because web site operators whose sites are targeted as containing undesirable content can simply change their web site address; and an Internet user in a country imposing controls can simply dial into a server outside the country and access the desired information, thereby avoiding the proxy server altogether. An "Anti-Censorship Proxy" has been created that allows users to evade filters. Even if the telephone company is state-owned, it cannot differentiate a telephone call to a foreign server from an international fax. Furthermore, encryption allows determined users to create "tunnels" to banned foreign sites in ways that completely evade government control. And while access through an Internet Service Provider is desirable, dial-up access is available from any telephone that can make an international call.

Access to the Internet can also be wireless, making it even harder for governments to exercise controls. The creation of mirror sites is one practice that helps assure the free flow of information, even against government censorship efforts. Given the global nature of the Internet, content can be published from anywhere in the world. When a government tries to prosecute a content provider or force the withdrawal of material, there are others around the world prepared to copy or mirror the information on their own sites, in countries where the information is legal. One example involved the site of a Basque organization hosted by an American service provider. The site was supporting Basque independence, although it did not promote violence. Nonetheless, from Spain, there came an apparently orchestrated campaign of "mailbombing" — flooding the site's service provider with e-mail in order to disrupt service. The service provider publicized the problem and soon a number of organizations, one in Holland, one in England, several in the U.S., installed mirror websites, which were perfectly legal in the host country. With so many sites, the harassment campaign fizzled out. The Internet Freedom Campaign, an English group hosting one of the mirror sites, set up an on-line bulletin board for surfers to post their opinions about the issue, showing how the Net is the perfect place for controversial information to appear, Similarly, when a local governmental body in the UK, the Nottinghamshire County Council, sought to suppress the publication of the so-called JET Report, an official report on the hysteria that has attended certain child abuse cases, the report was immediately mirrored on numerous sites, ultimately totaling 35, as a result of a campaign organized by GILC member Cyber-Rights & Cyber-Liberties (UK), When an issue of a Zambian newspaper carrying an article critical of the government was banned, the issue was mirrored outside the country.

Despite the power of the Internet — or perhaps because of that very power — governments have sought to restrict it. Government actions infringing freedom of expression on the Internet take many forms:

— *Internet-specific laws:* Some governments have criminalized certain types of speech on the Internet. Such criminal penalties may come in the form of laws whose expressed intent is to protect minors from certain material regarded as "harmful." However, as the United States Supreme Court recently found, requiring that Internet speakers shield certain populations from their speech is effectively a total ban on that speech.

— *Application of existing laws:* Governments can act to restrict speech without specifically enacting laws targeting Internet-based speech. For example, German government action against CompuServe for providing access to material illegal under German law did not require enactment of new law, merely the assertion by government agents that certain Internet speech violated the existing laws.

— *Content-based license terms applied to Internet users and service providers:* Several countries have already established licensing systems that require Internet users and/or service providers to agree to refrain from certain kinds of speech, or block access to speech as a condition of having a license to use the Internet or provide access to the Net. China has issued rules requiring anyone with Internet access to refrain from proscribed speech. And the Singapore Broadcasting Authority requires all Internet Service Providers to abide by licensing terms demanding that they block access to foreign web sites and newsgroups deemed harmful to national morals.

— *Compelled use of filtering, rating or content labeling tools:* Blocking, filtering, and labeling techniques can prevent individuals from using the Internet to

> exchange information on topics that may be controversial or unpopular, enable the development of country profiles to facilitate a global/universal rating system desired by some governments, block access to content on entire domains, block access to Internet content available at any domain or page which contains a specific key word or character string in the address, and over-ride self-rating labels provided by content creators and providers. Where any such mechanisms are required by public authorities or otherwise forced on users, they constitute serious threats to human rights.

Over the past half-century, international human rights law has enshrined the rights to free expression, access to information, and privacy of communications, creating a strong presumption against governmental intrusions. These rights are reflected both in the provisions of numerous international and regional agreements and in decisions rendered by human rights tribunals. These human rights doctrines protecting freedom of expression are fully applicable to the Internet. Indeed, these protections may offer especially strong protection to the Internet, given its unique features. These human rights instruments have their limitations.

The Universal Declaration has been accepted in effect by all 185 Member States of the United Nations, but not all of its provisions have become binding. The International Covenant on Civil and Political Rights is binding, but its enforcement mechanisms are limited. While there are binding regional agreements for the Americas, for Europe, and for Africa, there are none for Asia or the Middle East. Enforcement mechanisms are available under these regional agreements, but they are limited too. Where individual review is available, the time required to pursue a case all the way to the international level may be substantial. Most importantly, these instruments, particularly the European Convention, are burdened with exceptions that have been seriously criticized as over-broad. Nonetheless, these human rights agreements have served to expand freedom of expression worldwide, becoming part of international law and affecting the domestic laws of many nations.

The advent of the Internet raises the question of how these human rights instruments apply to the new communications media. The answers are in some respects encouraging: the instruments are drafted with very forward-looking language, with powerful implications for a medium that operates "regardless of frontiers."

The international community has stated its commitment to the right to free expression in a series of fundamental agreements, including the Universal Declaration of Human Rights, the International Covenant on Civil and Political Rights, and the International Covenant on Economic, Social and Cultural Rights.

The right of free expression was first proclaimed an international norm by the then-members of the United Nations in the 1948 Universal Declaration of Human Rights ("Universal Declaration"). Taken together, Articles 19, 12, and 27 of the Universal Declaration constitute a blueprint for the protection of free expression on the Internet.

Article 19 of the Universal Declaration proclaims: "Everyone has the right to freedom of opinion and expression; this right includes freedom to hold opinions without interference and to seek, receive and impart information and ideas through any medium and regardless of frontiers."

Article 12 of the Universal Declaration provides: "*No one shall be subjected to arbitrary interference with his privacy, family, home or correspondence.*" The language of this provision is broad enough to encompass all communications directed to an individual or group of individuals, including electronic mail and newsgroup communications. Finally, the right to seek, receive and impart information guaranteed in Article 19 of the Universal Declaration is reinforced by Article 27, which upholds the right of each individual "*freely to participate in the cultural life of the community, to enjoy the arts and to share in scientific advancement and its benefits.*" Given that the Internet's roots are in the exchange of scientific information, Article 27 seems particularly apt to the protection of communications on the Internet.

The foresightful language of Article 19 ("*through any medium*") makes it clearly applicable to expression via the Internet. The rights to "seek" and "impart" information seem particularly relevant to "surfing" the 'Net and posting information on Web sites for all to read, while the right to "receive" information encompasses the exchange of electronic mail and the downloading of information.

The Universal Declaration is subject to exceptions. Article 29(2) provides:

> "In the exercise of his rights and freedoms, everyone shall be subject only to such limitations as are determined by law solely for the purpose of securing due recognition and respect for the rights and freedoms of others and of meeting the just requirements of morality, public order and the general welfare in a democratic society."

The Universal Declaration is not a treaty. It was adopted by the United Nations General Assembly as a resolution having no force of law on its own. However, over time the Declaration has become a normative instrument that creates some legal obligations for Member States of the UN. Many of the principles established by the Universal Declaration have since entered the corpus of international law as evidenced by an overwhelming consensus of opinion and practice among states. This consensus is illustrated in subsequent international and regional treaties and agreements, decisions of international tribunals, and domestic constitutions and legislation. Further, the Declaration has served as an inspiration for other human rights agreements of more direct effect.

The United Nations Commission on Human Rights was created in 1946 under Article 68 of the UN Charter. States name representatives to the 53 member Commission, where they serve as instructed governmental delegates. The Commission prepares reports and coordinates an expansive network of working groups and rapporteurs with thematic or country mandates. It has been criticized for being politically motivated and selective in approach, but it serves as the principal UN forum for addressing charges of human rights violations and as a focal point for broadening the human rights agenda of the UN. In 1993, the Commission established the position of Special Rapporteur on the promotion and protection of the right to freedom of opinion and expression. In his 1998 report to the Commission, the Special Rapporteur specifically commented on the impact of new communications technologies and governmental efforts to regulate them:

> "The Special Rapporteur is of the opinion that the new technologies and, in particular, the Internet are inherently democratic, provide the public and individuals with access to information sources and

> enable all to participate actively in the communication process. The Special Rapporteur also believes that action by States to impose excessive regulations on the use of these technologies and, again, particularly the Internet, on the grounds that control, regulation and denial of access are necessary to preserve the moral fabric and cultural identity of societies is paternalistic. These regulations presume to protect people from themselves and, as such, they are inherently incompatible with the principles of the worth and dignity of each individual. These arguments deny the fundamental wisdom of individuals and societies and ignore the capacity and resilience of citizens, whether on a national, State, municipal, community or even neighbourhood level, often to take self-correcting measures to re-establish equilibrium without excessive interference or regulation by the State."

In its resolution of April 1998 on the right to freedom of expression, the Commission welcomed the Special Rapporteur's report and specifically invited him to "assess the advantages and challenges of new telecommunications technologies, including the Internet, on the exercise of the right to freedom of opinion and expression,... taking into account the work undertaken by the Committee on the Elimination of Racial Discrimination on racism, racial discrimination, xenophobia, and related intolerance."

The principles first enunciated in the Universal Declaration are reiterated and expanded upon in the 1966 International Covenant on Civil and Political Rights ("ICCPR"), which took effect in 1976 and has now been ratified by 140 nations. Article 19 of the ICCPR restates Article 19 of the Universal Declaration almost verbatim. It declares: *"Everyone shall have the right to hold opinions without interference. ... Everyone shall have the right to freedom of expression... ."* In words somewhat more expansive than the Universal Declaration, Article 19 of the ICCPR expressly states that the freedom of expression extends to all forms of media: *"this right shall include freedom to seek, receive and impart information and ideas of all kinds, regardless of frontiers, either orally, in writing or in print, in the form of art, or through any other media of his choice."* The ICCPR also reiterates the crux of Article 12 of the Universal Declaration: *"No one shall be subjected to arbitrary or unlawful interference with his privacy, family, home or correspondence."*

The ICCPR defines the scope of limitations that could be imposed on the freedom of expression. Consistent with the law of most if not all nations, the ICCPR recognizes that freedom of expression may be curtailed under certain circumstances. The ICCPR requires, however, that restrictions on free speech be narrowly defined and not arbitrary. Article 19(3) of the ICCPR provides that restrictions on the freedom of expression are valid only where such restrictions are *"provided by law and are necessary: a. For respect of the rights or reputation of others; [or] b. For the protection of national security or of public order, or of public health or morals."*

The essence of applying the ICCPR involves interpreting this limitation. It has been urged that this provision means that laws restricting freedom of expression must be "accessible, unambiguous, drawn narrowly, and with precision." Moreover, the burden of demonstrating the validity of a restriction on free speech should lie with the government. The key hurdle for governments is the requirement that restrictions be "necessary;" this has generally been interpreted as a high standard. The ICCPR includes several other provisions relevant to freedom of expression. Article 17 provides,

"No one shall be subjected... to unlawful attacks on his honour and reputation. ... Everyone has the right to the protection of the law against such... attacks." Article 20 states, *"Any advocacy of national, racial, or religious hatred that constitutes incitement to discrimination, hostility or violence shall be prohibited by law."*

Under the Covenant, States Parties are required to submit reports every five years on the measures they have taken to protect and advance human rights. The Covenant established a Human Rights Committee, one of the principal functions of which is to examine these reports. The Committee makes conclusions on individual state reports and also issues general comments, which serve as advisory opinions on the Covenant. (The Committee also has had since its inception jurisdiction over complaints filed by one State Party against another, but few states declared their acceptance of the mechanism and it has never been used). In 1976, an optional protocol went into force which enables private parties to file individual complaints against States Parties that have ratified the covenant. The protocol is itself a treaty, and therefore binds the states that have ratified it. Complainants must exhaust domestic remedies first. Once a complaint has been admitted as properly drawn, the Committee brings the matter to the attention of the state involved, which has six months to respond. The Committee, after considering all the written communications on the matter, issues its "views." The Committee has no power to enforce its findings, but it does require States Parties to indicate in their periodic reports what measures they have taken to give effect to the Committee's recommendations. "In particular, the State Party should indicate what remedy it has afforded the author of the communication whose rights the Committee has found to have been violated."

Restrictions on the Internet also implicate rights established by the International Covenant on Economic, Social, and Cultural Rights ("ICESCR"). Echoing Article 27 of the Universal Declaration, Article 15 of the ICESCR recognizes the important *"benefits to be derived from the encouragement and development of international contacts and cooperation in the scientific and cultural fields."* Accordingly, the 136 signatories pledge to *"diffuse science and culture"* and to *"respect the freedom indispensable for scientific research and creative activity."* These provisions articulate that free expression across borders must be respected to realize social, scientific, and cultural advancements. To take advantage of such progress, Article 15 of the ICESCR establishes that all individuals are entitled "to enjoy the benefits of scientific progress and its applications." One of the most effective means of doing so is through Internet communication, which enables people in distant and diverse countries to share valuable scientific research and social insights. The ICESCR does not establish any interstate or individual complaint system. It only requires the States Parties to submit *"reports on the measures which they have adopted and the progress made in achieving the observance of the rights recognized herein."* Art. 16(1). There is a Committee on Economic, Social and Cultural Rights, which reviews the country reports and issues General Comments and analyses, which serve as a platform for the Committee to try to advance awareness of human rights issues arising in the social context.

Regional human rights agreements in Europe, the Americas, and Africa establish the right of free expression for all individuals and privacy in their communications with others. Such freedoms are protected in all forms of media and "regardless of frontiers." These regional agreements are especially important because of the opportunities they offer for international judicial review of actions restricting free expression. The European Convention for the Protection of Human Rights and Fundamental Freedoms ("European Convention") was adopted in 1950 by members of the Council of Europe. Article 10 states in full:

— "Everyone has the right to freedom of expression. This right shall include freedom to hold opinions and to receive and impart information and ideas without interference by public authority and regardless of frontiers. This Article shall not prevent States from requiring licensing of broadcasting, television or cinema enterprises.

— "The exercise of these freedoms, since it carries with it duties and responsibilities, may be subject to such formalities, conditions, restrictions or penalties as are prescribed by law and are necessary in a democratic society, in the interests of national security, territorial integrity or public safety, for the prevention of disorder or crime, for the protection of health or morals, for the protection of the reputation or rights of others, for preventing the disclosure of information received in confidence, or for maintaining the authority and impartiality of the judiciary."

The European Convention thus establishes that the right of free expression pertains to cross-border communication, which naturally applies to much of the content available on the Internet. Closely linked to freedom of expression are additional rights in the European Convention: the right to respect for correspondence and privacy, contained in Article 8; the right to freedom of peaceful assembly and freedom of association, contained in Article 11; and the right to manifest one's religion or belief, contained in Article 9. Article 10 is not stated in absolute terms. The second paragraph specifies that freedom of expression can be curtailed in furtherance of a series of enumerated interests. It has been widely debated whether these exceptions are too broad. But even in the U.S. and other countries with constitutional free speech provisions, restrictions are permitted through judicial interpretation. Supporters of Article 10's approach argue that Article 10 is preferable because the catalogue of possible restrictions is limited and because Article 10 also establishes that any restriction on the exercise of the freedom of expression must be "prescribed by law" and "necessary in a democratic society" to serve one of the enumerated interests.

Application of the exceptions in the second paragraph will always turn on the factual and legal context, considered case by case. In specific situations, it has been found that there was no violation of Article 10 in: the application of blasphemy laws to seize a film, the UK's ban on broadcasting interviews with representatives of the IRA, prohibitions on Nazi material, laws against obscenity, even state disciplinary measures against a lawyer who used aggressive or insulting language. Article 10 must be interpreted in light of other Articles, notably Article 17, which states that nothing in the Convention creates a right to engage in activities *"aimed at the destruction of any of the rights or freedoms set forth in the convention."* Article 17, it has been held, was intended "to prevent totalitarian groups from exploiting, in their own interests, the principles enunciated in the convention." Accordingly, for example, the Court has concluded that it was not a violation of the Convention for the Netherlands to convict extremist right-wing Dutch politicians for distributing racist leaflets. Other provisions affecting the freedom of expression include Article 6, which guarantees the right to a fair trial, and the right to personal privacy in Article 8, which protects a person's honor and reputation against attack, both of which concepts are also reflected in Article 10(2) itself.

Most European countries that are party to the Convention have made it part of their national law, meaning that it can be invoked in the national courts. For many years, the UK declined to do this, but the Convention will be fully incorporated in UK law when the Human Rights Bill 1998 is enacted. The European Convention has an explicit enforcement mechanism based on judicial review by an independent regional tribunal, the European Court of Human Rights, located in Strasbourg. The most important feature of the Court's jurisdiction is that individuals can bring complaints against Contracting States alleging violations of the Convention. The procedures of the Court are well beyond the scope of this paper. It is sufficient to note that individuals may bring their cases before the Court after exhausting local remedies and that an application must first be presented to the European Commission on Human Rights.

The Commission decides on the admissibility of the complaint. If the Commission decides that the case is admissible, it issues a report (which is not binding), and there is a procedure for referring cases to the Court. The Court's judgments on the merits are binding but declaratory in nature. The Court has no power to quash the impugned decisions of the national authorities. The Court may, however, award "just satisfaction" in the form of financial compensation. In most cases, States have been reasonably swift to make the changes in their laws and practices necessary to bring them into conformity with the Court's decision.

European countries also manifested their commitment to free speech in the Council of Europe's 1982 Declaration on the Freedom of Expression and Information ("Council of Europe Declaration"). This Declaration reaffirms Article 10 of the European Convention and proclaims that the freedom of expression is *"a fundamental element [of] the principles of genuine democracy, the rule of law and respect for human rights."* The Declaration also provides that the freedom of expression and information is *"necessary for the social, economic, cultural and political development of every human being, and constitutes a condition for the harmonious progress of social and cultural groups, nations and the international community."*

The Council of Europe Declaration thus recognizes that the freedom of expression serves not only an individual interest, but the interests of nation states and the international community as well. Significant in the context of Internet communication, the Council of Europe Declaration recognizes that *"the continued development of information and communication technology should serve to further that right, regardless of frontiers, to express, seek, to receive and to impart information and ideas, whatever their source."* To achieve this high level of protection, the Council of Europe member states agreed to the following objectives:

— "absence of censorship or any arbitrary controls or constraints on participants in the information process, on media content or on the transmission and dissemination of information;

— "the availability and access on reasonable terms to adequate facilities for the domestic and international transmission and dissemination of information and ideas; [and]

— "to ensure that new information and communication techniques and services, where available, are effectively used to broaden the scope of freedom of expression and information."

The 55-member Organization for Security and Co-operation in Europe ("OSCE"), formerly known as the Conference on Security and Co-operation in Europe, sponsored the 1990 Charter of Paris for a New Europe. Signed by 31 countries from Europe, Russia, Canada, and the United States, the Charter proclaims: "*We affirm that, without discrimination, every individual has the right to freedom of thought, conscience and religion or belief, [and] freedom of expression.*" The OSCE's 1994 Budapest Summit Declaration, "Towards a Genuine Partnership in a New Era," complements the Charter by asserting that participating members "*take as their guiding principle that they will safeguard*" *the right to freedom of expression and recognize that "independent and pluralistic media are essential to a free and open society.*" The Internet is the most "independent and pluralistic" of all media; it should therefore benefit from the strongest protection against restrictions on the free flow of information. OSCE member states also have committed to making "*efforts to facilitate the freer and wider dissemination of information of all kinds [and] to encourage co-operation in the field of information.*" In accordance with this commitment, and in recognition of commitments made under the Universal Declaration and the ICCPR, the OSCE declared that its member states "*will ensure that individuals can freely choose their sources of information.*"

Countries of the OSCE reaffirmed the ICCPR's limitations on the scope of permissible restrictions on the right of free expression. The 1990 Conference on the Human Dimension concluded that any restrictions on fundamental rights and freedoms must be

1) provided by law;
2) consistent with obligations under international law, particularly those made pursuant to the ICCPR and the Universal Declaration; and
3) must relate to one of the objectives of the applicable law and be strictly proportionate to the aim of that law.

Regional agreements from the Americas also explicitly embrace the freedom of expression. The American Declaration of the Rights and Duties of Man was the first international human rights instrument, predating even the Universal Declaration. Article IV of the American Declaration states: *"Every person has the right to freedom of... expression and dissemination of ideas, by any medium whatsoever."* The American Convention on Human Rights ("American Convention") was adopted in 1969 and entered into force in 1978. It is worth quoting in full, for several of its provisions are of particular relevance to current debates concerning the Internet:

— "Everyone has the right to freedom of thought and expression. This right includes freedom to seek, receive, and impart information and ideas of all kinds, regardless of frontiers, either orally, in writing, in print, in the form of art, or through any other medium of one's choice.

— "The exercise of the right provided for in the

foregoing paragraph shall not be subject to prior censorship but shall be subject to subsequent imposition of liability, which shall be expressly established by law to the extent necessary to ensure:

a. respect for the rights or reputations of others; or

b. the protection of national security, public order, or public health or morals.

— "The right of expression may not be restricted by indirect methods or means, such as the abuse of government or private controls over newsprint, radio broadcasting frequencies, or equipment used in the dissemination of information, or by any other means tending to impede the communication and circulation of ideas and opinions.

— "Notwithstanding the provisions of paragraph 2 above, public entertainments may be subject by law to prior censorship for the sole purpose of regulating access to them for the moral protection of childhood and adolescence.

— "Any propaganda for war and any advocacy of national, racial, or religious hatred that constitute incitements to lawless violence or to any other similar action against any person or group of persons on any grounds including those of race, color, religion, language, or national origin shall be considered as offenses punishable by law."

The American Convention has several features that go beyond other human rights instruments. For one, the American Convention explicitly states that the exercise of the right of freedom of expression *"shall not be subject to prior censorship."* The rule against prior censorship is also reinforced by Article 14, which provides for a right of reply by anyone inured by inaccurate or offensive statements or ideas disseminated to the general public. In a provision that may be relevant to the problems posed by Internet "self-regulation," the American Convention applies to private action and makes it clear that the right of expression may not be restricted by indirect methods or means. Article 13(3) provides that the *"right of expression may not be restricted by indirect means, such as the abuse of government or private controls over newsprint, radio broadcasting frequencies, or equipment used in the dissemination of information, or by another means tending to impede the communication and circulation of ideas and opinions."*

The American Convention, in language identical to the ICCPR, sets forth a list of permitted grounds for restriction, a list narrower than that in the European Convention: restrictions on speech must be *"expressly established by law to the extent necessary to ensure [either] [r]espect for the rights or reputation of others... or [t]he protection of national security, public order, or public health or morals."* Article 11 of the American Convention, like other international agreements, protects the privacy of personal communications: "No one may be the object of arbitrary or abusive interference with his private life, his family, his home, or his correspondence."

The protections of the Convention are enforced by the Inter-American Commission on Human Rights and by the Inter-American Court of Human Rights. The Commission is an institution of the Organization of the American States. It has the authority to conduct investigations and make recommendations to both the OAS and to Member States. It can "prepare such studies or reports as it considers advisable in the performance of its duties." It can issue advisory opinions to governments. And it is required to take action on petitions by individuals or NGOs and "communications" by Member States. The Inter-American Court of Human Rights is the principal judicial organ of the inter-American system. Only the Commission and the States Parties have standing before the Court; individuals cannot directly institute proceedings. The Court hears cases of an adjudicatory (or "contentious") nature and also can issue advisory opinions. Proceedings are instituted by the filing of an application either by a State Party or by the Commission. An individual wishing to bring his or her case before the Court must file at the Commission (after exhausting domestic remedies). The Commission then takes the case to the Court

The Inter-American Court has noted that the American Convention is more generous in its guarantee of freedom of expression than the corresponding provisions of both the European Convention and the ICCPR. The Court stated in one case: "Freedom of expression is a cornerstone upon which the very existence of a democratic society rests. It is indispensable for the formation of public opinion. ... It represents, in short, the means that enable the community, when exercising its options, to be sufficiently informed. Consequently, it can be said that a society that is not well-informed is not a society that is truly free."

One of the leading opinicns of the court has to do with the indirect means of controlling freedom of expression, and specifically with a form of self-regulation. The Compulsory Membership case involved a United States citizen who was working in Costa Rica as a journalist without being a member of the Association of Journalists as required by Costa Rican law. He was convicted of the illegal exercise of the profession of journalism in the absence of membership in the Association. The Court said that any restrictions on the freedom of expression must meet four requirements: the existence of previously established grounds for liability; the express and precise definition of these grounds by law; the legitimacy of the ends sought to be achieved; a showing that these grounds are necessary to ensure the ends.The Court placed considerable emphasis on the requirement of necessity, in terms that have relevance to attempts to censor the Internet.

Following the rulings of the ECHR, the Court concluded that necessity implied the existence of "a pressing social need." It was not enough to demonstrate that the regulation was simply useful, reasonable or desirable. The necessity and hence the legality of restrictions "depend upon a showing that the restrictions are required by a compelling governmental interest." Furthermore, the court held that in accordance with the principle of proportionality, the restriction must be "closely tailored to the accomplishment of the legitimate governmental objective necessitating it." The Court noted that the Inter-American Convention prohibited private controls on the freedom of expression. It indicated that the type of private controls prohibited by the Convention might arise when monopolies or oligopolies instituted practices that restricted speech. The association of journalists was another form of private control, albeit one backed up by a law compelling membership.

In defense of the rule, it was argued that compulsory membership was the normal way to organize a profession in order to guarantee adequate standards, thus better serving the community. The Court found this argument unpersuasive. In order to demonstrate that the restriction was necessary, it had to be shown that the same results could not be achieved by less restrictive measures. The Commission in a 1994 report adopted and reiterated the principles expressed by the court. The Commission proceeding involved "desacato" laws, which criminalized expression that offended, insulted or threatened a public official in the performance of his or her duties. The Commission found that such laws did not serve a legitimate purpose and were not necessary. The Commission also adopted a test similar to the Brandenburg test in the united States, stating that "criminalization of speech can only apply in those exceptional circumstances when there is an obvious and direct threat of lawless violence."

In the past, it was assumed that a country could control content within its borders, subject to free expression principles, and that publishers had some ability to control and direct the distribution of their materials. Thus, in *Handyside*, even though the book at issue was legal in most countries of Europe, Article 10 of the European Convention was not violated by the UK's efforts to prohibit its sale in the UK. If a restriction was justified in a particular country, then it applied to both domestically produced and foreign produced material, even if the foreign material was legal where produced. A magazine printed legally in the Netherlands would have to be tested by German standards if someone wanted to distribute or possess it in Germany. But this margin of appreciation doctrine — clearly in tension with the language "regardless of frontiers" — was based in large part on the physical nature of the media by which information and ideas were produced and disseminated. Respect for differing legal norms — even though freedom of expression was raised to the level of an international right — was based on the premise that a country had a reasonable chance of success in keeping material out of its territory, at least things like books or reels of film or paintings on canvas, and that publishers had a reasonable chance of success in controlling distribution of their materials. On the Internet, neither governments nor publishers have this type of control over information, for information is no longer tied to physical objects.

The global nature of the Internet should give new relevance to the concept "regardless of frontiers" found in human rights instruments. As Judge Martens said in a separate opinion in the Spycatcher case, "in this 'age of information' information and ideas cannot be stopped at frontiers any longer." Judges Pettiti and Farinha made the same point in their separate opinion: "In the era of satellite television it is impossible territorially to partition thought and its expression or to restrict the right of information of the inhabitants of a country whose newspapers are subject to a prohibition."Under human rights principles, expression on the Internet will still be subject to restriction, but without the "margin of appreciation" that has supported restrictions in so many cases.

The Internet requires the adoption of a true international standard of review, one that must look to consensus rules generally. The rise of the Internet also requires a reexamination of the meaning of the concept to "seek and receive" and to "impart" information. National restrictions on local speech have a direct and negative impact on the ability of Internet users around the world to "seek and receive" information and ideas, as well as their right to "impart" information. For example, if citizens of one country are prohibited from discussing political issues critically online, then not only are their rights infringed upon, but also the right of others around the world to "seek and receive" that information is directly implicated. Similarly, a country's efforts to block certain content from outside its border implicates the right of those in other countries to "impart" the information.

Internet Service Providers (ISPs) play a special role in the operation of the Internet. While ISPs differ in nature from country to country, most people most of the time access the Internet through an ISP. The crucial role ISPs play in providing access to the Internet has made them the target of some governments' efforts to regulate content on the Internet. Those countries have assumed that if they can control ISPs, they can control content on the Internet. ISPs do not fit any of the existing media paradigms. They are very distinct from broadcasters. For this reason, it is not legitimate to subject them to regulatory structures designed for other technologies. There are two sets of arguments against making ISPs responsible for content they do not create. First, trying to make ISPs responsible for information that flows over their systems (but which they did not create) would fundamentally change the nature of the Internet and could destroy its power. Second, there is growing recognition that ISPs cannot technically assume responsibility for content they did not create. The task of sifting information is impossible. It would be so easy to encrypt content, to change addresses, to send images by email.

Technical factors prevent a service provider from blocking the free flow of information on the Internet. First, an Internet service provider cannot easily stop the incoming flow of material. No one can monitor the enormous quantity of network traffic, which may consist of hundreds of thousands of emails, newsgroup messages, files, and Web pages that pass through in dozens of text and binary formats, some of them readable only by particular proprietary tools. As the European Commission noted recently, "it is as yet unclear how far it is technically possible to block access to content once it is identified as illegal."A second technical problem is that a provider cannot selectively disable transmission to particular users. Electronic networks typically do not allow for the identification of particular users or their national region. ISPs cannot provide material in one country while blocking it in another; such a distinction would require an enormous new infrastructure on top of the current network. Some networking technologies, such as newsgroups, may allow individual operators to select some groups or items and block others. But many technologies, such as the World Wide Web, currently do not support such selectivity.

A number of countries have recognized, after considerable study and debate, that ISPs should not be liable for content they did not create. This reflects a judgment that while ISPs ought to provide law enforcement reasonable assistance in investigating criminal activity, confusing the role of private companies and police authorities risks substantial violation of individual civil liberties. In 1997, Germany adopted a Multimedia Law (the Information and Communications Services Act) which provides that access providers are not responsible for any third-party content to which they only provide access. Providers also are not responsible for "any third-party content which they make available for use unless they have knowledge of such content and are technically able and can reasonably be expected to block the use of such content." In the United States, section 230 of the Communications Act, 47 United States

Code sec.230, states "No Provider or user of an interactive computer service shall be treated as the publisher or speaker of any information provided by another information content provider." In adopting this provision, Congress specifically found that "the Internet and other interactive computer services offer a forum for a true diversity of political discourse, unique opportunities for cultural development, and myriad avenues for intellectual activity," and it said that its goal was "to promote the continued development of the Internet."The European Commission also has concluded that regulation of ISPs was not the best way to address content regulation. In its 1996 Communication to the European Parliament, The Council, The Economic and Social Committee and the Committee of the Regions on Illegal and Harmful Content on the Internet, the Commission stated that "Internet access providers and host service providers play a key role in giving users access to Internet content. It should not however be forgotten that the prime responsibility for content lies with authors and content providers."

The Commission stated that blocking access at the level of access providers would go far beyond the limited category of illegal content and "such a restrictive regime is inconceivable for Europe as it would severely interfere with the freedom of the individual and its political traditions." Therefore "the law may need to be changed or clarified to assist access providers and host service providers, whose primary business is to provide a service to customers."Therefore, the position of the ISPs should be clarified, and they should not be targeted by the individual governments and law enforcement bodies where the ISPs have no control of the Internet content."

The European Parliament in its decision of 13 May 1998 and the Council of The European Union in it recommendation of 28 May 1998 both agreed with the Commission and concluded, in effect, that ISPs should not be liable for content they did not create. The "Bonn Declaration" of European Ministers likewise underlined the importance of clearly defining the relevant legal rules on responsibility for content of the various actors in the chain between creation and use. The Declaration recognized the need to make a clear distinction between the responsibility of those who produce and place content in circulation and that of intermediaries such as the Internet Service Providers. In the EU and in a number of other countries, "self-regulation" has been offered as a viable alternative to governmental control of Internet content. The use of the term "self-regulation" is a misnomer in the context of controlling speech on the Internet. In the normal sense of the phrase, "self-regulation" is when a group of people or companies decide that, in their own best interest, they should themselves regulate how they go about their joint interests.

However, what is being suggested by the term "self-regulation" as applied to the Internet is not that ISPs as a group should regulate their own behavior, but rather that ISPs should regulate the behavior of their customers by taking down offensive websites or blocking offensive content. Under international law, privatized control may be harder to challenge. However, in a number of cases, it may be clear that the ISP is acting under pressure from the government and has, in essence become the agent of the government for carrying out a government policy. What is often promoted as Internet "self-regulation" is actually "privatized censorship." It is consistent with the fairly common occurrence of having a formerly direct government function turned over to a private business. The backing is still state power and government threat, but the actual implementation and mechanics of the suppression of material is delegated to a trade group. GILC member Cyber-Rights & Cyber-Liberties (UK) wrote in its report "Who Watches the Watchmen: Internet Content Rating Systems, and Privatised Censorship" "The current situation at the UK does not represent a self-regulatory solution as suggested by the UK Government. It is moving towards a form of censorship, a privatised and industry based one where there will be no space for dissent as it will be done by the use of private organisations, rating systems and at the entry level by putting pressure on the UK Internet Service Providers. One can only recall the events which took place in the summer of 1996 and how the ISPs were pressured by the Metropolitan police to remove around 130 newsgroups from their servers."

When ISPs come together to self-regulate certain classes of content in exchange for some limit on their liability for that content, the overwhelming tendency will be to censor more material, rather than less, in an effort by the ISPs to be certain that they have removed any material that might be illegal. Where ISPs are dependent on government grants of liability limitations, their "self-regulating" actions must satisfy the perceived demands of law enforcement, even if this results in removal of legal, protected speech.Initial reports from "self-regulatory" systems cast doubt on their effectiveness and suggest that the only effective way to combat crime such as child pornography is with well trained police. The two most important hotlines in Europe, the Dutch hotline and the UK hotline, have observed that despite the large amount of complaints they receive, this amount is tiny compared to the vast volume available on the Internet. The effects these hotlines have on dissemination of illegal content is also tiny. The Dutch Hotline, in its annual report, warned that it had absolutely no effect on distribution of illegal content in chat-boxes and E-mail, and that its influence on such distribution in newsgroups was very limited. According to the Internet Watch Foundation Annual Report, of the 4,300 items blocked by private action, "[o]nly the few articles appearing to have originated in the UK are suitable for investigation and action by the UK police." Thus with little measurable law enforcement impact, thousands of presumably legal items were nevertheless removed from the Internet. Blocking, filtering, and labeling techniques can restrict freedom of expression and limit access to information when used or mandated by governments or their agents. Specifically, such techniques can prevent individuals from using the Internet to exchange information on topics that may be controversial or unpopular, enable the development of country profiles to facilitate a global/universal rating system desired by governments, block access to content on entire domains, block access to Internet content available at any domain or page which contains a specific key-word or character string in the URL, and over-ride self-rating labels provided by content creators and providers. Government-mandated use of blocking, filtering, and labeling systems are subject to the same limitations under basic international human rights protections as other Internet restrictions.

7

E-Finance for Development

The advent of online electronic finance has brought with it the promise of cheaper, faster and more widely available finance for small and medium-sized enterprises (SMEs). Various types of online financial services that may be available to SMEs have already emerged or are coming on stream. The Internet is a global phenomenon and so is e-finance. Its deployment is not limited to developed countries, and indeed some developing countries - such as Brazil, India and the Republic of Korea - are experiencing particularly strong growth in e-banking.

It is interesting to note that, to a large extent, although the initial impetus has often been provided by foreign institutions, local financial institutions have now successfully taken the relay. In many developing and transition economies the local enterprise sector has also developed active Internet and e-commerce strategies, thus matching the e-finance drive of the local financial service providers. The dynamics of e-finance in emerging economies, while not dissimilar, are clearly not identical to those of e-finance in the developed countries. It appears that by and large, e-finance in developing countries is driven by Internet banking, e-payments, and e-trade finance. Activity in financial markets is still limited, although in countries such as Mexico and the Republic of Korea online brokerage services appear to be quite well developed. On the other hand, some e-financial services seem to be specifically tailored to the developing and transition economies. This is the case of microfinance, which will be discussed in the section on SMEs' specific services.

This chapter begins with a review of current trends in e-finance, including Internet banking, e-trade finance and e-credit information, and then looks at the global e-finance platforms. It also provides a review of SME-related e-finance experiences and initiatives in developing countries and, finally, outlines the challenges facing SMEs and related players.

Documentation on e-finance for SMEs is still heterogeneous and fragmented, especially regarding developing and transition economies. In particular, there is a lack of information on the attitudes of users of e-finance services. E-finance suppliers provide a large share of the available documentation.

However, in some cases the information is provided to support business initiatives and therefore the data should be used with caution. This chapter is based on published data and information made available by experts participating in two recent UNCTAD e-finance related events, namely the UNCTAD Expert Meeting on Improving Competitiveness of SMEs in Developing Countries: Role of Finance, Including E-Finance to Enhance Enterprise Development, held from October 22 to 24, 2001 in Geneva, and the UNCTAD Side Event "E-

Finance for Development", held on 19 March, 2002 in the framework of the International Conference on Financing for Development convened by the United Nations in Monterrey, Mexico.

Throughout the chapter, a narrow definition of e-finance - to mean financial services delivered online through Internet fixed and wireless networks to enterprises and households - will be used. However, where appropriate, the discussion covers related areas such as the offline use of electronic devices for payment transactions in remote areas.

Internet banking

Internet banking refers to the deployment over the Internet of retail and wholesale banking services. It involves individual and corporate clients, and includes bank transfers, payments and settlements, documentary collections and credits, corporate and household lending, card business and some others.

Since its inception Internet banking has experienced strong and sustained growth. According to Jupiter Media, Internet traffic for all United States banks grew by 77.6 per cent between July 2000 and July 2001, compared with overall World Wide Web traffic growth of 19.8 per cent over the same period.

Another source estimated that the share of United States households using Internet banking will increase from 20 per cent in 2001 to 33 per cent in 2005, and that by 2010 there might be 55 million users. In France, the number of online banking accounts is recording an annual growth rate of 75 per cent and is forecast to reach 10 million by 2003. Datamonitor forecasts that between

2000 and 2003 the number of online bank accounts in Europe may grow annually by 34 per cent, increasing from 14.3 million in 2000 to 34.2 million in 2003.

Internet banking operations currently represent between 5 per cent and 10 per cent of the total volume of retail banking transactions both in the United States and in Europe. This is less than the share of Internet securities trading, estimated at between 20 and 25 per cent of the total, but much more than overall business-to-consumer (B2C) e-commerce, which represents less than 2 per cent of the total retail trade.

Internet banking is becoming a driving force shaping the future of the banking industry. All banks, including those that were cautious in the past, intend to offer access to their products and services via the Internet, which is seen as a major distribution and communication channel. The current status of Internet banking shows that - contrary to what some analysts initially expected - pure Internet banks have gained only a limited share of the market. In fact, the traditional banks have not been destroyed and, while a few of the pure Net bank models may succeed, no newcomer has been able to penetrate the banking sector on a large scale.

The "click and mortar" model - a strategy combining physical and Internet presence - has thus become the dominant model. The traditional banks and other financial service providers have adopted aggressive Internet strategies. At present the entry barriers to Internet banking appear to be much higher for new entrants than was the case during the early days of this type of banking.

The barriers stem from customer attitudes and the very nature of banking services and products. The traditional banks with a strong customer base have a competitive advantage over newcomers. However, to maintain this advantage is not easy. The key to success is to keep abreast of technological change and sophistication; this allows a bank to understand the potential of Internet technologies and to integrate them into a coherent business strategy.

For many banks the scale of the requisite operations and investments creates problems of outsourcing or aggregation of services. For "click and mortar" banks, transforming bank branches into multipurpose advisory centres would also encourage clients to move to Internet banking, since the majority of Internet users also make use of bank branches and automated teller machines (ATMs). The idea is to transform bank branches into "one-stop shops", i.e. well-networked financial advisory centres for clients. Thus the prevailing model of Internet banking today is the one that is thoroughly integrated within the existing banking infrastructure, which combines click and mortar systems.

To further develop e-finance, banks need to show customers that they provide the same security standards on the Internet as in traditional banking. Moreover, like credit card associations and companies, banks should assume, at least in the initial stages, full responsibility for covering the costs incurred by clients as a result of a security breach and unauthorized transactions. To encourage migration to Internet banking, the banks should also offer better interest rates and cheaper accounts. The ability to gain customers' trust thanks to security, willingness to take responsibility and the offer of financial incentives has been an important feature of the most successful pure Net banks.

Many global financial service providers have developed specialized SME-related Internet banking. For example, Citibusiness, a service of Citigroup, provides online various e-finance services to SMEs, including current, savings and money market accounts and certificates of deposit. Furthermore, SMEs can apply online for lines of credit, loans and mortgages. The service also includes the management of clients' funds in separate accounts. Other global players, such as HSBC, Deutsche Bank, Standard Chartered Bank are also developing similar services.

Payment systems, particularly the wholesale systems used for transactions among financial institutions, have been moving to an electronic infrastructure since the beginning of the 1970s. Electronic payment systems and networks were based on proprietary protocols and dedicated telecommunication infrastructure.

The Internet has radically changed this situation. It is an open network infrastructure, involving direct non-hierarchical links between the buyer, the vendor and any intermediaries, as well as between them and the technology providers. The Internet model dissociates the network from the physical infrastructure. It allows interconnection between heterogeneous networks and provides ubiquitous common standards, whose development is no longer controlled by a single entity or even a group of entities. Furthermore, with encryption technology, digital certificates and smart cards, it is now possible to provide security in a modular and flexible fashion. Thus a highly secure environment can be created on the public networks.

The Internet entails a radical value shift, although this view is not necessarily universally shared. Even leading players such as SWIFT and Visa have not yet transferred their core operations to open systems, and this creates a degree of uncertainty as far as their future operations are concerned. For many payment systems, use of Internet Protocol standards and protocols does not entail a radical change in their business practices and their governance. It remains to be seen whether the full advantages of Internet architecture can be gained without fully accepting the open network model.

Despite numerous attempts aimed at offering innovative alternatives, credit and debit cards and their existing payment network and procedures are still the main payment instruments for B2C transactions. They are used in more than 90 per cent of online purchases. Small businesses are using them for some of their payments. However, there is a broad recognition that the current credit-card-based payments cannot fully satisfy e-commerce transactions. Most e-tailers consider the current payments structures to be quite expensive. Even the supposed beneficiaries of this situation, namely banks and payment networks, do not particularly like those structures. The card networks point out that Internet transactions represent a disproportionate percentage of charge-backs and fraud.

To make payments more secure and to reduce merchant's liabilities for fraud and certain charge-backs, Visa introduced the so-called Verified by Visa (VbyV). It is hoped that the introduction of such applications will increase consumer confidence in Internet-based card payments. At the same time, card-based payments are not yet well suited for either small-value (micro-payments) or large-value payments. Whether the recently introduced smart cards combining the virtues of all cards and other e-banking characteristics (in a chip embedded in a card) will make cards suitable for micro- and large-value payments remains to be seen.

In order to find an alternative to card-based system, a number of alternative Internet payment initiatives have been launched. The first-generation systems (including initiatives such as Digicash, Cyber Cash and Cyber-com) were wound down after encountering severe problems. Micro-payments, which were also considered in the mid-1990s to be a viable mechanism for transactions of intangible goods (information, online entertainment and others), have not taken off as expected, at least not yet.

The main problem with these first-generation Internet payment initiatives is that they were not focused enough on their customers' behaviour and attitudes. Most of them appeared to be hasty steps in the search for more efficient and lasting solutions. They combined considerable technological sophistication with a degree of marketing and business naivety. They also became trapped in a vicious circle: merchants would not offer e-payment schemes if few customers used them, while customers would not use e-payments if few merchants accepted them.

Despite the poor record of the first wave of e-payment schemes, the development of Internet-based payment has not slowed down but instead has broadened in scope. Online payments continue to attract new entrants, including cyber-entrepreneurs backed by venture capital and well-known IT providers such as Microsoft and Yahoo. The range of proposed solutions is becoming wider and currently includes, virtual points providers (e-centives.com, mypoints.com), P2P (peer-to-peer) payments (PayPal, BillPoint, PayDirect, eCount.com), virtual escrow systems (escrow.com, tradesafe.com), digital wallets (Yahoo Inc., Microsoft Passport), virtual and smart cards (Visa, American Express, Mastercard), and electronic bill payment and presentment or EBPP (e-route, billserv.com, Check-Free Transpoint).

The multiplicity of online payment methods reflects the continuing search for standards in the industry. Moreover, online payments devices are now becoming more diversified by moving from PC workstations to mobile devices and Internet enabled television sets.

One of the successful payments solutions with the potential to organise online payments for small SMEs and microenterprises is Paypal. While still relying on traditional banking accounts and card infrastructure for actual fund transfers, it has managed to capture from the card associations the online P2P payments market. The payment architecture of Paypal combines innovation - the use of e-mail for payment notification and confirmation, account management and its integration into existing payment systems.

Using existing networks Paypal plays the role of a merchant by keeping the books of e-mail transactions as its own and settling a large proportion of them. Paypal's income is derived primarily from the float on accounts, which it manages, complemented by fees charged to purchasing customers and service providers. This business model allows Paypal to undercut the traditional merchants, particularly for small businesses. This arises, for instance, in the context of online auctions, where buyers and sellers need a sure, secure and cost-effective payment mechanism to settle their transactions. Paypal has also benefited from having a close association with the leading cyber-auction operator, E-Bay (25 per cent of E-Bay payments go through Paypal). A system such as Paypal can capitalize on viral marketing, as each user of Paypal encourages his or her friends and business acquaintances to open an account.

While payments card associations such as Visa, Mastercard and American Express were already at the forefront of Internet based payments (and are now moving towards their further diversification), the banking industry was also changing its attitude - from being reactive to proactive. The creation of Identrus and the migration of SWIFT, the most important global interbank payments network, to the Internet under the SWIFTNet programme were among the most visible examples in that respect.

The largest payment card association, Visa has continued to experience a spectacular growth in its payments traffic. Between 1985 and 1997 Visa transactions increased from $100 billion to $1 trillion; they then doubled, reaching $2 trillion in 2001 (Visa International 2002). However the share of e-commerce related payments is still low and concentrated mainly in the B2C sector. While continuing to upgrade its e-payments modules based on PC workstations, Visa is exploring new payment devices such as mobile phones, palms and computers (m-payments), Internet powered TV sets (t-payments), offline payments between electronic devices in proximity (p-payments) using infrared or Bluetooth technologies, and payments initiated by voice sensitive technologies (v-payments).

As far as SME servicing is concerned, Visa has developed several solutions, including Visa Business (permitting SME buyers to have a short-term trade credit limit embedded in the limit of a given card), Visa Distribution (permitting large wholesale suppliers to automate the account receivables from SME buyers), Visa Purchasing (permitting larger enterprises to streamline procurement process) and Visa Commerce (a non-card-based B2B payments model). Such models are inter alia helping to integrate SMEs into online payments and in particular familiarizing them with larger company standards.

Visa and other card companies were among the leaders in developing a critical technology of the smart card. This technology has been used in South Africa, for instance, to create financial infrastructure for people without banking accounts. In the medium term, the smart card might provide secure and cost-effective support for specialized payment and settlement services, inter alia for SMEs, including those operating in the informal sector.

The SWIFT network is a core element of the global payment infrastructure. Like Visa, it is experiencing an impressive growth in the volume of its operations. From 1991 to 2001 SWIFT message traffic increased from less than 0.4 billion to 1.5 billion messages a year. Daily traffic in 2002 peaked at close to 8 million messages a day. Most SWIFT payments are directed towards Europe, while Fedwire continues to dominate payments in the United States.

SWIFT has cooperated with European central banks to support their real-time gross settlement systems, serving as a common messaging service for the majority of high value payment systems in the euro zone. Its role in providing market infrastructures is also expanding, as it is becoming a messaging hub for clearing and settlement in securities, using Global Straight Through

Processing (STP), and in foreign exchange trading, using Continuous Linked Settlement (CLS) systems, which are in its turn linked to Real -Time Gross Settlement (RTGS) one.

From the standpoint of the global payment infrastructure, the December 2000 decision of SWIFT to migrate to a new IP-based network, SWIFTNet, represents a major milestone.

It is expected that SWIFTNet will combine IP standards with highly secure, high-performance networks, owned and operated by SWIFT. The principal SWIFT application, FIN, starts to migrate to SWIFTNet from August 2002 and will form SWIFTNetFIN, a fully IP based application. As a result, all SWIFT customers will have to migrate to the Internet.

It is expected that SWIFTNet will offer a wide range of other services, including information, security and payments. SWIFTNetFIN's ambition is to become the infrastructure of choice for the new generation of Internet technologies based payment systems and related services.

To run the above-mentioned systems requires nearly 100 per cent security standards. Many security arrangements have been proposed in order to achieve such a result. The most notable arrangement is Identrus, a United States based organization created in early 1999 and owned by 42 global financial institutions, which act as Identrus Certificate Authorities for corporate customers in more than 133 countries.

Identrus seeks to create a global trust infrastructure, based on Public Key Infrastructure (PKI) enabling business-to- business (B2B) commerce among all companies using this infrastructure. The Identrus network will link in a structured and hierarchical way various security and certification systems created by its member banks. The Identrus itself will operate a root certificate authority (root CA), an entity at the pinnacle of the electronic identity hierarchy. Identrus' legal and technical infrastructure is based on a set of uniform system rules, contracts and business practices for comprehensive trust and risk management (UNCTAD, 2001).

In December 2000, four major banks - ABN AMRO Bank, Bank of America, Deutsche Bank and HypoVereinsbank - joined with Identrus and deployed trust-enabled B2B applications. In 2000, Identrus announced a strategic alliance with SWIFT. The introduction of IP standards will allow SWIFT members and users to have single interfaces with various infrastructures and services.

Transactions in denominated notes are still the main payments method for SMEs. Although handling cash is extremely expensive and cash balances do not earn interest, cash is still used even in developed countries. For example, at the end of 2001, the total amount of United States dollars in circulation was around $620 billion (i.e. $2,200 per capita). Even if one assumes that 75 per cent of that amount was used abroad there is still $550 per capita for United States residents. The scale of cash transactions is higher in Europe and even more so in Japan, not to mention the developing and transition economies. In developed countries the ratio of payments to gross national product (GNP) is very high, but in developing countries it is much lower; this indicates that in those countries money circulates less rapidly and that there are lower levels of formal financial intermediation.

The need to participate in e-commerce and the requirements for entering the chain of online payments are constantly pushing SMEs to adopt the culture of online payments. Similarly, the increasing shares of online retail and wholesale payments in overall payments are generating increased SME participation in online payments.

Some of the above-mentioned payments systems, mainly B2C, could also be adapted to SME and microenterprises requirements. At the same time B2B payments methods are also making inroads. Medium-sized and large enterprises are seriously considering using electronic invoice presentment and payment (EIPP, a B2B cousin of EBPP) in inter-enterprise payments. According to experts, online EIPP cuts costs related to online handling of accounts receivable (AR) and accounts payable (AP) in comparison with their paper versions, by more than half. In the European Union and in many other countries, since digital invoices are now legally acceptable, it is possible to process EIPP and EBPP.

In many cases these systems are run by banks, to which enterprises outsource their receivables and payables activities. The reason for outsourcing is the reluctance of enterprises to make large investments while establishing those systems in-house. Also, outsourcing enables them to cut even further the costs related to handling the e-invoices traffic.

Most SMEs, especially in developing countries, still operate mainly in their national markets. However, this should not prevent them from using the Internet for payments. In fact, the Internet's main use - as far as e-payments are concerned - is for domestic payments. For example, in 1999 domestic payments represented 99 per cent of the volume and 86 per cent of the value of all payments transactions. According to a projection by Boston Consulting Group, while between 1999 and 2009, international payments might experience high growth rates and could increase from $238 trillion to 510 trillions, their share in overall payments will probably increase by 3 per cent, from 14 to 17 per cent. The same consulting group projects much higher growth rates for domestic payments in developing and transition economies during the same decade.

According to a World Bank survey, the average online banking penetration for developing countries by the end of 1999 was close to 5 per cent. For some countries, the penetration was considerably higher and growing rapidly. At the same time, according a survey by Citibank, United Arab Emirates, user preferences related to banking channels are as follows: bank branch - 12 per cent; ATM - 0 per cent; Telephone banking - 0 per cent; online web based banking - 76 per cent; mobile phones - 12 per cent. In other words, the developing countries are also voting for Internet banking.

In Brazil, the number of e-banking users reached 8 million in 2001 and is growing rapidly. Most Brazilian banks have followed the click and mortar strategy and also entered into strategic alliances with leading Internet service providers (ISPs).

Thus Banco Itau entered with AOL into an agreement to bring its customers to AOL services offering free access and customized features facilitating access to e-banking. Today, the majority of the leading Brazilian banks, including Banco do Brazil, BNDES, CEF, Bradesco and Banco Itau are offering advanced e-banking services and nearly a quarter of their client base has already migrated to the Internet. Moreover, SMEs are active users of online banking. Thirty per cent of Banco Itau SME customers are operating online. Unlike in Argentina, Brazilian banks have managed to preserve the real value of their customers' deposits in spite of a period of high inflation rates.

As a result, with a high level of banking intermediation (65 per cent of the population) Brazilian banks have espoused Internet banking, which has been well received by both consumers and enterprises, while dollarization and disintermediation in Argentina created a demand side problem for banks and thus discouraged them from investing in Internet banking. At the same time, increased insecurity in the streets due to social unrest or crime is prompting many users to opt for Internet banking, so as to avoid physically visiting a bank. Thus the crisis in Argentina led to a short-term increase in the use of Internet banking.

Mexico is another leader of Internet banking in Latin America. It adopted legislation providing for the development of both e-commerce and e-finance. One of the local leading banks - Banamex - has over 1.25 million users of Internet banking, including 50,000 companies, mostly SMEs. The Mexican subsidiary of the Spanish bank BSCH has launched P-market, an online market place linking SMEs with various suppliers. The bank offers online functionalities to allow SMEs to manage their finance online, and has developed an online procurement system, called Procura Electronica. The bank experienced a rapid increase in the number of its online clients in the first year of operation.

India, one of the leaders in software development, has an advanced online banking system. Over 50 banks offer online services. The example of the largest private bank, ICICI Bank, is really impressive. It has multiplied by four the number of its online banking users, who represent over 15 per cent of the total. Its SME department is a leader in the design of wholesale e-finance credit lines for Indian SMEs.

E-banking permits business process re-engineering to achieve zero latency leading to improvements in customer service levels and better risk management because of real-time settlement. While the argument for drastically reducing transaction costs is more debatable in India owing to low e-banking adoption rates, low labour costs and "free" existing branches, there is a better price discovery process as more and more markets gain integrated real-time and improved access to these trading and data-dissemination platforms. At the same time, however, many changes are still required in technology, access infrastructure and banking regulation.

In Bangladesh there is a large gap between the computerization of foreign banks and that of local commercial banks (the gap is particularly great in respect of local public commercial banks) and as regards the state of their intra- and inter-branch online networks.

However, 75 per cent of local banks are planning to introduce e-banking, which implies very dynamic improvements in their ICT use indicators. Virtually all banks use banking software at their head offices and during the past few years around one third of local banks has become SWIFT members.

Credit card and point of sale services (POS) are already provided by a quarter of local banks, while ATM and internet banking are expanding rapidly especially in major cities.

In regions lacking adequate telecommunication infrastructure, technologies that make it possible to store and transact value in proximity and offline are taking root. Thus smart cards based on Visa Horizon proximity technologies are being introduced in Ghana and some other African countries.

The Visa Horizon and Visa Electronic systems could be of particular interest to microenterprises in remote rural areas. In countries with low banking penetration or where there is mistrust towards local banks, the establishment of basic ATM cards for employees, issued by well-known payment card companies, makes it possible to cash salary cheques, and this represents a step towards establishing banking relationships inter alia through e-banking.

Finally one of the most impressive records has been achieved by the Republic of Korea, which has higher than the OECD average e-commerce and e-finance indicators. Internet banking in that country has increased at a rapid pace, the number of online users having risen from 2 million in 2000 5.3 million in December 2001. The country is a leader in the region with 54 per cent of users having multiple online banking relationships.

The Republic of Korea is also leading in online brokerage and in mobile banking. In South-East Asia Internet banking is also developing rapidly in Thailand, Malaysia, Singapore and to a lesser extent, in the Philippines. Apart from North and South Africa the Sub Saharan Africa is the region that is seriously lagging behind in Internet banking, although it is giving to the rest of the world the good example of microfinance developments.

Electronic trade and finance systems

Designed to facilitate the movement of goods and services, trade finance systems rely on complex flows of complicated and traditionally paper-based documents, and this makes the whole process slow, costly and error-prone. Hundreds of billions of dollars are being spent annually on processing the paperwork associated with international trade.

For several years, various participants in international trade have sought to simplify the process and migrate from paper-based to electronic documents. This task has been laborious and often frustrating because of the difficulties in defining common standards.

The advent of Internet technologies has the potential to significantly accelerate the progress towards fully electronic trade finance. However given the fact that trade finance related payments are only a small part of the overall payments traffic, the banks have had to make hard choices either to retain trade payment and finance functions for themselves, or to outsource them and save on transaction costs while keeping the client base.

The need to outsource trade services was the main reason for industry-wide, private initiatives to create global online platforms centralizing the servicing of the trade cycle and in particular the trade finance part. Those platforms have the potential to service the trade and trade finance needs of SMEs. The following is an outline of Bolero, Tradecard and CCEweb.

Bolero International Ltd. is a United Kingdom based joint venture of SWIFT and the TT Club (an association of freight insurers) created in April 1998. The aim was to create a platform for the secure electronic transfer of commercial trade documentation and data worldwide via the Internet. The platform went live in September 1999, with SWIFT operating the system under contract to Bolero.

Bolero maintains that it acts as a neutral and trusted third party that provides the so-called Core Messaging Platform for highly secure delivery and receipt of all trade related electronic documents and payments. In addition to a common technology platform, bolero.net provides a unified legal structure that binds together all parties involved in international trade (importers, exporters, shipping agents, freight forwarders, customs and international banks).

The messages between users are validated and acknowledged while the Title Registry application facilitates, online, the transfer of ownership of goods. After extensive consultation with the industries, Bolero issued a Rule-Book, which allows disputes to be resolved in the same way as with paper documentation. In addition Bolero allows for the application of the provisions of eUCP, the electronic version of Uniform Customs and Practice for Documentary Credits (UCP) of the International Chamber of Commerce (ICC). Bolero has also developed a value- added service called SURF, which matches trade documentation online between buyers, sellers and banks in order to accelerate all trade transactions and reduce error rates.

At present, SWIFT operates the Core Messaging Platform on behalf of bolero.net. It is planned to be one of the first services to migrate to SWIFTNet. In order to demonstrate its commitment to Internet technologies and their tangible benefits, Bolero and its users have developed BoleroXML, a set of specifications which describe the standard structure and contents of the electronic version of a common trade document such as Commercial Invoice, Bill of Lading and Packing List. UN/CEFACT has recently endorsed Boler-oXML as a migration path to the ebXML standard. Bolero is committed to providing an open solution that runs over the Internet.

TradeCard is a United States company developing an online substitute for the traditional bank-based letter of credit (L/C). It intends to make it a trust building platform for the process of online negotiations in trade transactions and related payments. It was launched in 1997, and went live on the web in 2000 (for more details see UNCTAD, 2001).

TradeCard focuses on what is often considered a critical bottleneck in international trade transactions: lack of an inexpensive and efficient system for cross-border trade payment settlement. In March 2001, Trade-Card introduced an automated, collaborative, global trade settlement platform which is intended to streamline and automate the processing of virtually any payment transaction, whether it is domestic or cross-border, guaranteed or open account, large or small.

Initially, the banks were reluctant to accept the new competitor. But currently TradeCard works with a dozen international banks and has entered into strategic partnerships with Coface as payment insurer, Marsh, the largest broker of cargo insurance, Master-Card and Thomas Cook, as well as with Cap Gemini Ernst & Young.

CCEweb is a Canadian company, which has based its @GlobalTrade - an electronic payment and trade management system - on the eUCP and existing trade services banking infrastructure. The company launched its initiative in September 2000 and has built strategic partnerships with Adobe, CGE&Y, China Systems, Identrus, SITPRO and Visa International. While retaining the existing rules and banking practices to which the trading community is accustomed, it tried to create simplified electronic versions of a letter of credit as well as streamlining the flow of electronic trade related documents.

CCEweb states that it has developed arrangements to streamline operations for both exporters and importers. It hopes that the banks will find its centralised platform a useful tool to outsource costly L/C related operations. While it did not challenge the existing practices on L/C unlike Trade-Card, and did not create a parallel rules book unlike Bolero, it did try not only to adapt those instruments to the Internet, but also to develop easy and fast-track versions of e-L/Cs.

The @GlobalTrade system allows the printing of the original electronic bill of lading and other trade-related documents in countries without enough technological capacity to cope with PKI solutions or legal and insurance structures to support them. CCEWeb also intends to start the use of passwords and pin numbers with clients especially from developing countries that do not yet have possibility to integrate into PKI systems. They will thus have electronic signatures. Passwords and pin numbers are especially important for developing countries' financial service providers and SMEs.

The systems claim to bring about major savings in costs and time through electronic processing of trade and especially trade finance documents. CCEweb might be the most user friendly one, while Bolero is the most secure one. At the same time alternative arrangements implemented by TradeCard introduce more competition into the system and push costs further down.

Bolero was an initiative of major financial industry players, while Tradecard and CCEweb are private ventures. Although all are now operational, none of them has yet become profitable. To remain operational, they still need financing, including venture capital financing and the issuance of new shares or debt financing.

Other companies active in facilitating cross-border trade payments via the Internet include LC Connect, Proponix, Actrade, FinancialOxygen, Qiva, Clear-Cross and Xign Corp.

Based in New York and in London respectively, ITFex and LTPTrade are B2B exchanges, created in 2000, that seek to develop an Internet-based secondary market for international trade finance instruments such as forfeiting bills, bankers' acceptances and shipping guarantees.

At present, this is an extremely fragmented and illiquid market, with an annual trading volume estimated at $75 billion in 2000. Celent Communications estimates that Internet technologies will stimulate the emergence of an electronic trade finance instruments market, whose value by 2005 should total over $700 billion.

At the same time, Celent recognizes that the growth of the electronic trade finance market will be slower than that of e-markets for other instruments such as bonds or equities. This is due not only to the disparate nature of trade finance instruments but also to the weaknesses of established automated trading mechanisms, such as matching, and of pricing benchmarks.

It is too early to judge the prospects of IFTex and LTPTrade, their development plans having been adversely affected by the general slowdown in B2B commerce. Both exchanges are now operational. In September 2001, LTPTrade launched a new release of its trade finance transaction and information platform. Key features of the new platform include improved offering and dealing functionality, as well as expanded research and information resources.

Emerging markets are expected to continue to be the main growth engine for the trade finance sector. Last year, trade finance flows between the United States and Western Europe diminished, wheras in Eastern Europe, Latin America and Asia, trade finance experienced high growth rates.

The total volume of L/Cs received by all Latin American exporters in 1999 reached $87billion, in addition to the $29 billion in documentary collections. Of this total, only $30 billion came from Latin America's trade with the rest of the world including the United States. Intra-regional trade is often made up of medium sized to large companies that lack open-account trade tools and rely on old-fashioned and expensive L/Cs.

This creates an opportunity for financial institutions seeking to offer electronic trade finance services. Banks such as Bradesco and Banco Itau in Brazil and Banamex in Mexico, seek to develop online wire transfers, online initiation of L/Cs, and other related online services. Sixty-five per cent of Mexican companies surveyed use at least one of the above mentioned products, and more than half of the companies in Mercosur countries turn to high-tech trade finance tools. Argentina used to lead in the proportion of companies using technology products

(58 per cent), but Brazilian companies use them more extensively than other Mercosur countries - 2.8 products on average per company in Brazil versus 1.7 products on average per company in the other countries.

However, local banks, large though they may be in their own country, suffer from a lack of global coverage. This explains their interest in global initiatives such as TradeCard and Bolero. Global banks such as Citibank, JP Morgan, Chase and ABN Amro are, of course, very active in this area and offer not only competitive pricing on trade financing products but also access to their networks and platforms. And when they cannot beat their local competitors, they co-opt them. In July 2001, Citibank bought Banamex for $12.5 billion.

In other parts of the world, e-finance trade initiatives are still in their early stages. In India for instance, Exim Bank, the German-based West LB and IFC (a World Bank affiliate) created in March 2001 a joint venture Global Trade Finance (GTF) Pvt Ltd to offer factoring and forfeiting services to Indian exporters. West LB has a 40 per cent stake in the venture, while Exim Bank has 35 per cent and IFC 25 per cent. In addition, the company has foreign currency lines of credit from both West LB and IFC, as well as a rupee line of credit from Exim Bank. GTF was set to begin operations in autumn 2001. One of its objective was to allow exporters to initiate their transactions online.

A more ambitious project, Global Trade Finance Network (GTFNet), seeks to facilitate the finance of trade debt receivables generated primarily from emerging markets, their acquisition and distribution worldwide. It is defined as a cross-territory extranet-based "business to business" network, with headquarters in Singapore and hubs in the United Kingdom, the Middle East and the Americas. Founded by Tara Kimbrell Cole and sponsored by a prestigious board, which is chaired by the former Chief Executive Officer of Standard Chartered Bank, GTFNet is not as yet operational.

Online credit insurance systems

The Internet provides a great deal of information about many companies through the use of search engines. However, relying on this source may not provide reliable information about risk. A proprietary credit information database on companies' performance, both as payers and suppliers, based on data from partners, experts, and actual transaction and debt collection experiences, is the type of source required to manage the credit and performance risks. Such Internet- based databases are run not only by banks but also by specialized agencies. Some of them are mainly credit information providers such as Dun &Bradstreet and Equifax, while others are credit insurers such as Coface and Gerling NCM.

In addition to providing credit information on companies, they cover traders' risks. Credit insurance is a less expensive alternative to bank-based letters of credit, which permits traders to rely on open account payment operations, thereby moving the counterparty risk to the credit insurer. Counterparty risk is particularly important in the case of SMEs, as their trade is often hampered by a perceived lack of creditworthiness or of a supply performance record, owing to the absence of reliable data and information about SMEs.

The Internet makes the collection of credit risk information easier but credit risk management tasks more complex. By reducing the cost of information and standardizing data formats, it makes it easier to gather and disseminate credit information. It also facilitates integration of information and transactions. At the same time, the Internet considerably expands the number of potential counterparties and the range of transactions.

Businesses active online have to deal with thousands of new buyers and sellers that they know nothing about. There is therefore a need for a quick and up-to-date creditworthiness assessments. The skills required for this activity are highly specialized and cannot be acquired overnight. Prior experience and accumulated historical data are essential. Barriers to entry are high. Not surprisingly, this segment continues to be dominated by a small group of suppliers, each of which has adopted an aggressive Internet strategy.

These strategies have common elements, for example all suppliers make their existing data available via the Internet, but there are also significant differences. Alternative approaches to credit information assessment, using innovative technologies, are also emerging. However, those approaches are being adopted and deployed by the existing suppliers rather than by new entrants.

Dun & Bradstreet (D&B) is probably the oldest existing provider of business information. It created the so called D-U-N-S Number (Data Universal Numbering System), which has become a standard for keeping track of millions of businesses in the United States. The system is also expanding worldwide. It provides identifiers of single business entities, while linking corporate family structures together. The D-U-N-S Numbers include parents, subsidiaries, headquarters and branches of more than 62 million corporate family members in 120 countries.

D&B is implementing a comprehensive Internet strategy to provide Internet-based services. Among those online services is D&B Global Access Toolkit, an online global data delivery service, and QuickBooks®, a business decision making tool for SMEs. D&B also seeks to become an important player in B2B e-commerce. To achieve this goal, the company entered into strategic partnerships with Oracle, Siebel Systems, SAP and other B2B players to integrate D&B products into their offerings.

In August 2001, VeriSign, Inc., the leading provider of Internet trust services and domain name registration services, and Dun & Brad-street announced an agreement under which e-businesses applying for VeriSign's Shared Hosting Security service will be automatically authenticated by Dun & Bradstreet using the company's global database.

The core business of Equifax is credit reporting, and enabling and securing global commerce. It has developed a range of diversified services, including transaction processing, direct marketing, customer relationship management and e-commerce security solutions. In July 2001, Equifax spun off its payment services into a separate company, Certegy.

Equifax's principal asset is the world's largest repository of consumer credit information. In January 2001, Equifax launched a new service - the Small Business Financial Exchange. Managed by Equifax, the Exchange brought together initially 15 of the largest United States small-business lenders - such as Bank of America, Bank One and Wells Fargo - in order to provide reports and maintain comprehensive trade data on small businesses. This has become a source of aggregated risk and exposure information on an estimated 25 million small businesses in the United States. The Exchange will enhance lenders' ability to make small business credit decisions and facilitate financing needs for this important segment of the economy.

Equifax Internet based products include Equifax Secure, Checkfree and SunTrust, which permit the identification and authentication of participants in online transactions. Another product, ePORT, tries to lower costs, speed up delivery and increase product penetration for the existing credit information services. Strategic alliances have been formed with Veri-Sign, Paymentech and PricewaterhouseCoopers.

The Coface Group, headquartered in Paris, is one of world leaders in export credit insurance and operates in 93 countries on five continents. Coface offers an integrated range of guarantees, including credit insurance, guarantee insurance, exchange risk cover and fidelity insurance, to its client companies worldwide. It also provides receivables management and credit information services. In order to allow its clients to analyse and monitor the financial position of their trading partners throughout the world, Coface has developed a Common Risk System, an online database containing information on 41 million companies, out of which 1.2 million are from developing and transition economies.

Coface has a credit exposure of $150 billion to 2.2 million companies, of which $15 billion i.e. 10 per cent, is the cover for companies from emerging economies. According to Coface, the overall performance of companies from emerging economies is not worse than that of OECD countries, which indicates the potential for enterprises from the emerging countries to access external finance and e-finance.

In December 1999, Coface launched a web-based rating system, @rating, that allows companies to insure trade debts and obtain credit limits online. The @rating system uses the data from the Common Risk System to develop a simple and easily accessible credit rating system, which allows a company to:

— Check a trading partner's reliability online;

— Protect transactions online. Apply for an @rating Quality Label and obtain a credit limit online;

— Check payment experience online.

@rating provides a method of assessing trade debts of less than six months' duration for amounts between 1,000 and 100,000 Euros, which represent the over-whelming majority of most traditional trade and e-commerce transactions. It offers a simple means for trading partners to protect themselves from the risk of default and to set customer credit limits, based on constantly updated information. For the first time, ratings are generated by an agency, which can in addition insure the risks it is rating. The Coface Group and its partners in Credit Alliance are backing the rating with a guarantee of payment, using credit insurance policies.

To facilitate its risk monitoring capability, Coface expanded @ratings to cover country risks. All Coface group products now incorporate the @rating solution. Since its launch, some 350 partners have integrated the @rating in their service offering.

Gerling-NCM (G-NCM) emerged at the end of 2001 as one of the largest global credit insurer after the merger of Gerling Namur with Dutch NCM. Gerling Namur was the result of the previous purchase of Belgian Namur by German Gerling. It has an active Internet strategy and its two main services are called E-Service and E-Trade. The E-Service permits the actual or potential insureds, brokers and other interested parties to access the G-NCM credit information database using the Internet based SERV@NET system. The database has information on company performance, policies and so forth. It is complemented by the group's Intranet called SERV@WORK, which gathers information on risks and is used as a tool for underwriting risks in all countries where G-NCM is present.

The E-Trade products represent various types of insurance cover. Those products include Trusted Shops, covering buyers from failed online shops (non-.delivery, non-refund, fraud etc.) and Trusted Trade, providing e-marketplace participants with credit insurance cover against the loss of receivables. Other insurance and financing products to render one-stop- shop financial services to those participants are also in the pipeline. They also include eCredible, in-sourcing online credit management services from companies and insuring their credit risks, for example verification of buyers, collection of receivables in time, credit monitoring and payment guarantee and Trade Cover, which offers online immediate coverage against risk of nonpayment of a buyer or group of buyers (it is not a comprehensive credit insurance against all buyers) and gives the insured a choice of protection level. The eCredible and Trade Cover are in some ways competing with the Coface @rating system.

It is important to note that credit information and credit insurance providers are not resolving the problems of market instability. While diminishing the risks of other companies' failures, they themselves could be exposed to the excessive demands arising from their obligation to insureds if their counterparties massively fail to respect contractual obligations in the event of a generalized economic crisis. In that case, credit information providers will find their prestige damaged because of the excessive number of errors in their judgement of credit risks, while the credit insurers might encounter difficulties in meeting their cover obligations even if their capital reserves meet the requirements of insurance regulators.

Many developing countries are following the examples of the United States and continental Europe by developing the necessary regulatory framework for setting up of credit information reporting systems. The essential elements of that framework include registration laws, bankruptcy laws, court registers; strict requirements for disclosure by private sector operators; public data dissemination and publishing requirements; the possibility of collecting, processing and disseminating public records, suits and judgements, and permission to access companies track records with banks for authorized institutions, etc.

However, the presence of credit bureaux in many countries does not guarantee the presence of exhaustive and updated data on SME payments behaviour and other key risk assessment data. The revolutionary impact of Internet data mining techniques in terms of coverage and reach, rather than transaction costs, could also boost the creation of a credit information industry in those countries, thus achieving a breakthrough in the risk assessments of a host of companies, including SMEs.

One of the most impressive examples of comprehensive credit information services in developing countries is Serasa of Brazil. Established in 1968 by Brazilian banks that realized there was a need to have a common risk data collection and assessment centre, Serasa today has the largest credit information data-bank on institutional and household borrowers in Latin America.

Receiving information from companies and households directly and also gathering information on them from independent sources (including court distributors, protest notaries, boards of trade, Central Bank, public registrars and official publications), Serasa contributes to the majority of decisions by banks, payment card companies and other financial service providers on extending credits to companies and households.

All products and reports of Serasa are available online. They include business behaviour reports, credit and analysis reports, and special SME reports. While Serasa has a very aggressive e-credit information programme to expand on the Internet it is also actively using other communications tools as fax, telephone and others.

Private equity mobilization

It is a widely shared misconception that, in the early stages of their existence, SMEs could raise capital from venture capital funds. On the contrary, those funds provide equity only to well-stablished SMEs with a good track record including good financials. Initial capital for a new business comes normally from the businessmen's own pockets or the pockets of their relatives, friends and so-called business angels - wealthy individuals ready to invest in the business plans, which are of interest to them.

Normally business angels are organized into associations. They support companies of their choice and pave the way for venture capital funds to invest. The latter take over SMEs having good chances to become large companies and in few years time further finance their expansion in order to prepare them for the initial public offering (IPO), i.e. selling their shares - and making, they hope, a large profit - on the well-established stock exchanges, where the firms become publicly quoted companies.

The Internet has introduced a new dynamism into the functioning of above institutions, permitting them in some cases to go for global initiatives and geographically diversify their portfolios. All large business angel associations and venture capital funds have functional websites where the SMEs. can look for interested investors by filling in the posted questionnaires and thus establishing initial contact with potential investors.

Linking private equity investors to SMEs in emerging countries is far more challenging than in OECD countries. With few exceptions such as Singapore, there is no local venture capital industry. And business angel networks are often family or ethnically based. Nevertheless, some efforts, spearheaded by international players, have been launched to create Internet-based private equity networks.

In January 2001, the United Kingdom's International Development Consortium (IDC) established a joint venture called Empower Link Holdings (Pty), with the

South African investment fund Omega. The idea was to take the EquityLink, its very successful business angel network created in 1995, into South Africa, linking it with United Kingdom and European opportunities. EmPower Link was supposed to provide support services to South African SMEs, including management development, financial management, business development, sales and marketing, IT, and innovation in technology and design. It was expected to contribute significantly to the development of a comprehensive SME support infrastructure in South Africa.

In February 2000, Softbank, one of world's best-known Internet companies, announced the creation of a joint venture with the International Finance Corporation (IFC) of the World Bank Group to establish start-up Internet companies in as many as 100 developing countries. The joint venture is an investment fund called Softbank Emerging Markets (SBEM), to be based in California's Silicon Valley on a capital base of $200 million. Seventy-five per cent of this will come from Softbank and the remaining 25 per cent from the IFC.

To begin with, SBEM will act as an incubator, investing in and providing advice to promising local Internet ventures in 10 to 20 countries. SBEM plans to establish a number of holding companies to make investments and oversee operations of local joint ventures in those countries. The first local office was opened in Malaysia.

Microfinance initiatives

Microfinance is an arrangement whereby microfinance institutions lend small amounts of money typically to a group of individuals or very small SMEs (with fewer than 10 employees). This process mainly happens within the framework of the informal economy, i.e. outside the formal financial system in developing countries and transition economies.

It is estimated that more than half of economic activities in sub-Saharan Africa derive from the informal economy. While the microfinance market requirements are estimated to be $300 billion, the assets of more than 8000 microfinance institutions worldwide do not exceed $7 billion. Keeping microenterprises out of the reach of the development community is unacceptable, considering the UN targets for the reduction of world poverty.

The approach here should be to consider the poor as an untapped resource rather than a social burden. Developing modern and inclusive microfinance actively using Internet technologies could help partly to implement this paradigm shift.

Pride Africa is a non-profit United States company with regional offices in Nairobi and operating activities in East and Southern Africa. It is one of the best examples in Africa of a successful and imaginative implementation of microfinance formulas with the active use of modern ICT technologies. With a network of 54 branches servicing more than 100,000 clients from Kenya, Malawi, United Republic of Tanzania, Uganda, and Zambia, Pride Africa has created a replicable franchise, including a proprietary software system, uniform operational processes and training for staff.

The financial and information service network provided by Pride Africa offers microfinance opportunities for local people and small enterprises that previously had no access to flexible financing, owing to rigid banking regulations and the information monopolies of government and large businesses.

The famous pioneer of microfinance, the Bangladeshi Grameen Bank, is also at the forefront of the efforts to bring e-finance to remote villages, using its microfinance services. By introducing POS terminals and diffusing smart cards in different villages it enables users to read and record entries, and to deposit and withdraw cash.

The Virtual Microfinance Market (VMM) is an information exchange system designed to facilitate interactions between microfinance institutions (MFIs), private investors, Governments and other participants in the microfinance market. It was developed by the United Nations Conference on Trade and Development (UNCTAD), with the guidance of an advisory board, and in the framework of a technical assistance project financed by the Government of Luxembourg.

VMM also provides contact and financial information on MFIs willing to mobilize commercial funding ("demand"), information on the legal and regulatory conditions of investment and links permitting direct contact with regulatory authorities in each country ("environment"). In addition, it also provides data on investors and financial intermediaries, information on conditions attached to past or current offers ("supply"), and access to sources of knowledge, technical advice and training in state-of-the-art techniques and tools for improving MFIs' financial management and access to capital markets ("knowledge").

This project is aimed at creating sustainable market links between the commercial investment world and the microenterprise sector in developing countries. It is expected to permit the investment on commercial terms, of millions of dollars at the grassroots level and the creation of thousands of jobs. VMM is accessible free of charge to all its members, i.e. to all duly registered information providers.

The above overview of enterprise related e-finance, while far from comprehensive, clearly demonstrates the breadth and the depth of e-finance development. The dotcom crash and the difficulties of B2B marketplace development over the last two years may have changed the public perception of the Internet and slowed somewhat the speed of its deployment but they have not changed the fundamental momentum of e-finance.

In the not too distant future the distinction between finance and e-finance might become somewhat blurred as the core financial technology, from user interface through middleware to applications and networks, will probably become Internet-enabled and Internet-based.

However, the process of evolution towards e-finance is still in its early stages. For one thing, Internet technology will continue to evolve towards larger bandwidth, fixed-wireless convergence and terminal access independence.

Beyond the technology, it is essential to understand the business dynamics of e-finance. On this score, it appears that there are four common misconceptions about e-finance, which help to explain some serious strategic errors, frequently committed by over enthusiastic promoters of e-finance.

There is no doubt that the Internet has the potential to reduce financial transaction costs. However, the cost reduction potential has often been exaggerated or misinterpreted. The cost dynamics of e-finance are quite complex. For one thing, in order to achieve the full potential of cost reduction, it is important to create a fully automated system, capable of straight-through processing. Such a system may require large investments in computing power, network building and programming capability.

Furthermore, the costs of migration from closed to open i.e. Internet-based architecture are often very high. For that reason, many e-finance enthusiasts favoured a "pure play" model, creating an Internet bank from scratch. The underlying assumption was that the newcomers had a crucial cost advantage. However, this assumption proved false. Whatever cost advantage newcomers may have achieved via technology, it was decisively undermined by the need for heavy client acquisition spending. Furthermore, while technology cost savings were often hypothetical, marketing costs were actual expenditures, amounting to between $150 and $300 per customer.

While such costs could be justified in online broking, this was not the case for Internet banking. The Internet did not invalidate the basic marketing rule that the cost of selling a new product to an existing customer is 10 per cent of the cost of selling to a new customer. A large part of Internet costs remain invisible at first glance, but they are still there.

A related fallacy was ease of implementation. While a basic website can be created cheaply and quickly, to design and implement a fully functional, industrial strength application capable of accommodating in a secure manner a large number of complex transactions and a huge variation in volume is a complex and protracted undertaking. In addition, there is limited previous experience to draw on and the necessary skills and know-how are still scarce. Thus, the potential for specification creep and cost overrun is as large with the Internet as it is in the traditional IT environment. This was vividly demonstrated by Vontobel Bank in Switzerland, which in spring 2001 announced a loss exceeding 120 million euros, due entirely to an overly ambitious Internet banking project.

Contrary to some high-profile pronouncements, the Internet economy is not frictionless. Actually, with a dramatic increase in the number of transactions and expansion of the universe of potential relationships, the overall level of friction is likely to increase. The abundance of information, opportunities and relationships increases the need for new intermediation structures and mechanisms. The challenge to the financial institutions and financial services providers is not disintermediation but the changing nature of intermediation. Thus, e-finance has stimulated the emergence of new categories of intermediaries such as financial portals, transaction aggregators and financial applications services providers.

Until 2000 it was commonly thought that e-business would revolutionize the financial industry and destroy the existing "dinosaurs." However, the evolution of e-finance clearly demonstrates the advantages of suppliers of established financial services, be they banking, transaction processing, credit information or insurance, as long they have the capacity to evolve and to embrace the new approaches and technologies.

The dominant business model today is "click and mortar" and an innovation is most likely to succeed if it is adopted by the leading players. This does not mean that financial services will not change, as they have been doing for the last few decades. Rather, the change will be more gradual and will probably take place mainly inside the established systems and structures.

While the dynamics of e-finance do not entail a sudden upheaval, it probably will lead to a profound and lasting transformation of financial services. Not only the access be broadened in terms of the number of potential users, but also these services will be available anywhere in the world, 24 hours a day, seven days a week. E-finance will enhance the information and technology content of financial services and thus further blur the boundaries between finance and technology, information and transaction, and financial institutions and technology providers. This evolution raises, among others, a number of substantive regulatory issues. In particular, banking, securities and insurance regulators should further strengthen cooperation within and between their groups at both national and international levels.

E-finance challenges for SMEs

Before engaging in e-finance, SMEs have to be already involved in e-commerce. Hence the e-commerce preparedness of SMEs is a measure of their readiness for e-finance. Although the Internet revolution was driven initially more by SME dotcoms than by large corporations, the majority of SMEs in traditional sectors are still lagging behind the large companies in the use of the Internet as a core element of business organization and a channel for developing e-commerce. Various surveys of SME e-preparedness in OECD countries suggest that only less than a quarter of SMEs with web presence actually use it as a business instrument, i.e. for the purpose of active web trading and related e-payments operations. In developing countries this indicator is much lower.

The majority of SMEs still limit their activities to maintaining a web page, with various levels of links and advertising. On the Internet they also gather information about markets and competitors, as well as searching for partners, with further negotiations taking place either through e-mails or offline, while successful deals are generally completed in a traditional manner, - that is, with traditional paperwork or through the use of cash.

According to some surveys, SMEs cite security concerns, lack of legal guarantees for online transactions, expenses related to hardware, software and maintenance, and the length and cost of training as the major impediments to starting e-commerce.

At the same time there is much less awareness in developing countries of the potential and importance of e-commerce. In that sense it is interesting to note the results of a Citibank survey of a sample of SMEs in Arab Gulf States (Saudi Arabia, United ArabEmirates, Kuwait, Qatar, Bahrain and Oman) and Middle Eastern or Mashreq countries (Egypt, Lebanon and Jordan) that inquired about their e-commerce preparedness.

While the majority of SMEs surveyed - 79 per cent and 73 per cent respectively - had access to the Internet, only 23 per cent and 38 per cent provided the Internet to all their departments, only 13 per cent and 18 per cent provided it to their procurement departments, and only 2.6 and 2.3 per cent had actually ever conducted online trading. Moreover, 45 per cent of Gulf and 25 per cent of

Mashreq SMEs did not have a positive approach to e-commerce, considering it less secure and of lower quality, and preferring traditional trade as a better business tool. In contrast, many SMEs in Latin America and Asia, and North and South Africa, do have access to the Internet. However, what matters is whether they consider it the tool for promising business models. Various surveys suggest that this is increasingly so for the majority of them.

The Internet provides SMEs with a unique opportunity to overcome economies-of-scale limitations by aggregating buyers and suppliers, i.e. linking individual SMEs to each other, to major companies, to e-procurement chains and to other e-marketplaces. For example, a Tunisian start-up, Intelligent DSP, works with the New Delhi office of Analog Devices to develop remote monitoring services for electrical power meters.

More broadly, successful e-commerce initiatives facilitate the emergence of new forms of business organizations such as virtual hubs and networks. By streamlining their operations and business relationships e-commerce helps to create a supply chain management for SMEs and overcome the high trade barriers they normally face. Increasing the role of buyer feedback helps to make production more customer- centred and flexible.

Creating many portals for SMEs with useful and functional contents greatly contributes to their efforts to access business information at much lower cost and hence to overcome the information asymmetry problem.

Among private sector efforts to facilitate SME access to e-business opportunities, mention may be made of the business portals specially designed to offer rapid and convenient answers to a variety of small business needs.

The challenge is to maintain a range of services that are both easy to find and effective. Banks have also launched SME-oriented business portals in order to ensure customer loyalty and create a basis for Internet- based banking services for SMEs.

Despite its recent slowdown, most analysts expect the B2B e-commerce market to grow substantially in the coming years. The Gartner Group forecasts that the worldwide B2B e-commerce market will reach $7.3 trillion by 2004. Initially, many B2B initiatives focused on so-called big-ticket deals among large enterprises, thus overlooking the great potential for SME involvement.

However, further changes are rapidly correcting this initial miscalculation. Efforts to involve SMEs more actively in B2B markets take two forms: adapting large exchanges to the specific needs of SMEs and developing specific exchanges for SMEs.

Although many SMEs see B2B markets as a way for large buyers to put additional pressure on suppliers to lower their prices, they understand the importance of emerging e-markets as supply channels for their products. As a result, many SME's are doing their best to adapt to the requirements of the global procurement platforms of large manufacturers.

The large e-marketplaces could cover a comprehensive range of B2B services for SMEs. That range includes supply chain management, e-procurement, SME's specific web service providers and exchanges. In particular, those bundled services might include web page creation, hardware and software integration and ISP connection, and low-end security products at affordable prices. One of the key problems of SMEs in the emerging economies is their unfavourable sectoral mix.

Most SMEs, which are active in traditional sectors, lack export capability. The lack of high-technology SMEs is certainly a major handicap for many emerging economies and an obstacle to the development of locally based e-commerce. On the other hand, the growth of the Internet provides an opportunity to create new businesses specializing in new technologies.

However, in order to realize this opportunity it is necessary to have access to technology and to create an environment capable of nurturing the new businesses. In the OECD countries, successful high-technology businesses are often concentrated (clustered) in small geographical areas, where they can obtain access to a wide range of resources, including technical skills, academic research, financial expertise and development know-how. More importantly, such clustering favours informal as well as formal contacts. Silicon Valley in the United States, Silicon Glen and Cambridge in the United Kingdom, Sophia Antipolis in France are often quoted as examples of high-tech clusters.

Such clusters also exist in developing countries such as India (Bangalore) and Malaysia (Penang). The transition economies are also trying to draw on their relatively developed workforce and education and R&D centres to accelerate the use of the Internet in their economic activities. At the same time other emerging markets are also trying to catch up.

Thus, recent projects in Africa and Middle East specifically oriented towards Internet-based technologies include El Ghazala in Tunisia, Gauteng Innovation Hub in South Africa and Internet City in Dubai. Given Dubai's role as major trade hub in the region and its liberal trade and investment regime Internet City may become a well-connected multifunctional technology hub. Many well-known foreign hi-tech companies have already opened offices there.

Support to SMEs is being provided at both international and national levels. In this connection, mention may be made of the G8 initiative (Global Marketplace for SMEs) and the EU initiative (Go Digital). There are many other initiatives by national Governments and other public entities.

Some of them are of a very general nature, while others are more specific, trying for example to create investors' networks, including business angels and venture capitalists for SMEs, or to provide access to the services of local export financiers (the United States Department of Commerce's Export Finance Matchmaker). Although many of them tend to overlap, they still cannot meet the huge demand from SMEs. Linking those networks together might help to do so. However, neither the Global Information Network for SMEs, nor the European Observatory of SMEs seems to have managed to create a network of networks devoted to e-commerce information for SMEs.

Although the developing countries also have their own programmes for modernizing SMEs, their capacities are much more limited. This makes it important for global and regional organizations, including the UN family, regional development banks, NGOs and others, to further expand their awareness-raising and technical and financial assistance activities in that field to support the SME sector in developing and transition economies. In this connection development of e-commerce with emphasis on SME needs is definitely part of the mandate of the ICT Task Force created by the UN Secretary

General. While it is hard to overestimate the advantages of the Internet for SMEs, it will require a great deal of awareness-raising and technical assistance from the international community to facilitate SME's participation in e-commerce.

E-finance includes Internet banking and payments, e-brokerage, e-insurance and other related services. Internet technologies have now penetrated all aspects of the financial services industry, including retail and wholesale, back office and front office, information and transaction. SMEs also use the bank lending and trade finance channels and are highly dependent on the quality of credit information related to their performance and financial health.

E-finance of immediate interest to SMEs in developing countries includes Internet banking and payments, e-trade finance, online credit information and related e-credit insurance and e-factoring operations. Microfinance shares a number of features with SME finance; it is also similar to household finance and can be considered to be a combination of both those forms of finance.

The e-commerce practices of SMEs in developing countries raise the question of their ability to gain access to Internet banking, online payments, online trade finance and Internet based credit information databases. In developing and transition economies there are many innovative initiatives to launch or facilitate e-finance for SMEs implemented by local banks, financial companies or other public and private sector based organizations and associations. The following are examples of some successful models and new initiatives.

SMEloan˜ SMEloan serves mainly the needs of SMEs in Hong Kong, China. The company offers Express Loans of up to HK$ 1 million, approved within one minute of submitting an online application. This allows business owners to obtain financing instantly. In practice, most SMEs borrow modest amounts. However, SMEloan offers possibilities of borrowing more than HK$ 1 million, using more time-consuming procedures.

The innovative approach of SMEloan was to finance SMEs with lower transaction costs and better results by leveraging Internet resources, thus making it possible to set up scalable lending operations based on knowledge of future cash flows, i.e. receivables of SME borrowers. By providing a home page to each borrower SMEloan requires borrowers to provide business data; these are automatically analysed by its risk diagnostic software, which gives early warning of any unusual operating trends manifested by the borrower. Only selected problematic borrowers are then addressed.

The others receive quasi-automatic credit approval similar to that given by a credit card company. In that sense, SMEloan is different from a bank that treats SMEs like other companies and hence incurrs higher unit costs from SME lending since it demands from SMEs complex sets of documents and assigns individual managers to each SME borrower. The successful SMEloan model attracted the attention of IFC of the. World Bank Group, which has invested $20 million in this promising venture.

Banks in many developing and transition economies are exploring possibilities of using online finance instruments to streamline the cash flow of SMEs on the basis, for example, of better management of their receivables, especially when the counterparts are the payables of large companies considered by banks to be much better risks. Here banks play the role of a factor discounting the receivables of SMEs.

The situation is more complex in the case of trade between SMEs. In this connection, credible and searchable live Internet based databases on SME risks initiated or created by SMEs associations themselves could be a solution. Moreover, the creation of mutual insurance funds by association members could serve to support bank's e-trade finance operations and thus reduce the level of their perceived risks.

An interesting initiative is the Smetrix B2B trade and e-trade finance clearing house proposal. Smetrix is a company in the Philippines that is trying to address the problem of more rapid and less costly access by SMEs to trade finance through the creation of a global e-sup-ply chain in which a central clearing house handles the problems of authentication and risk assessment of SMEs.

The clearing house, using its own database or partners credit information on SMEs, is expected to be able to create propitious conditions for SMEs either to have their online receivables discounted or receive structured finance (handling the risk of a given transaction) from a participating bank, or to securitize those receivables, capitalizing on the higher corporate rating grades of their trading partners.

Major players are apparently starting to support the idea of financial clearing house based on the Smetrix concept. According to Smetrix it is expected that General Electric will provide the necessary technology support, while IBM will provide the technology support for the clearinghouse and interfaces with banks. The HSBC Capital Markets service might take the lead in terms of developing a real-time trade financing system using large corporations with good credit risk ratings as anchors for enhancing the receivables of their SME suppliers.

At the same time Citibank might back- stop the electronic collections and settlements for those receivables, while Dun & Bradstreet through its Philippines subsidiary could deliver the online credit and evaluate the SME receivables.

The Small Business Guarantee Finance Corporation, which is the Philippine Government's financial institution ensuring financing and guaranteeing for SMEs, is committed to taking the lead in delivering guarantees on the receivables. It is interesting to note that the Philippine Central Bank considers supporting this type of SME access to e-finance to be a part of its microfinancing agenda.

While in some respects the system is reminiscent of Bolero, it has some distinctive features. Like Bolero, the Smetrix clearinghouse is intended to be a hub bringing together all trade related workflows and checking the authenticity of electronic documents. Also, it is expected to reconcile the contents of those documents, and this will permit online negotiations and confirmations between parties, thus facilitating the conclusion of deals and minimizing further disputes.

At the same time it is supposed also to be a constantly updated electronic library on credit information related to the trading participants. That library is intended to be constructed through the supply of information from partner banks and credit information and evaluating companies, as well as through the clearinghouse's record of trading partners' successes and failures.

However, the claim that a clearinghouse such as Sme-trix one eliminates risks is clearly an overstatement. While it can successfully handle the risks related to the authentication of partners or legal issues related to trade, it cannot fully control the risks related to the supply performance of the seller and the payment commitments of the buyer (in spite of mechanisms for upgrading credit risk). SMEs remain more vulnerable as trade partners because of their higher exposure to the vagaries of the economic cycle.

The positive signs related to e-finance for SMEs in developing countries include:

— The high level acceptance of technology by customers and financial institutions;

— The many innovative approaches;

— The initial tangible results in terms of market access and revenue generation.

However, most projects have not yet been launched on a large scale. It is therefore too early to determine which ones are likely to be the most successful and provide the "best practice" benchmarks to be replicated in other countries. Many aspects of the key question as to when and how e-finance will fundamentally change the conditions of SME's access to e-finance still remain to be resolved. Nevertheless, from the experience so far, a number of key challenges can be identified.

While Internet technologies are global and standardized, their applications can and need to be adapted to local circumstances. The Internet offers an amazing capability to reconcile global uniformity with local flexibility. It facilitates cross-border links, but at the same time creates new configurations of networks and clusters. Distinctions between proximity and remoteness remain highly pertinent, even if the distance becomes virtual rather than geographical.

The most successful e-finance stories in developing countries, including those of banks such as ICICI Bank of India, Banco Itau of Brazil and Banamex of Mexico, emphasize the ability to respond to local requirements in terms of product mix and delivery channels. The need to localize financial solutions is even greater with regard to e-finance for SMEs, which for the most part operate within a limited geographical area. Furthermore, their characteristics, size, financial structure and sectoral mix can vary considerably even within the same country or region.

Most e-finance developments have taken place through the interplay of competitive market forces, with limited public sector intervention. Some of them, particularly in Internet banking, have been launched by foreign institutions. The situation is quite different in the case of e-finance for SMEs, where public sector intervention is quite frequent. It is not only that the public authorities have to create the broad framework for e-commerce development (appropriate legislation and technological infrastructure, to mention the two most important) but also that they need to ensure that SMEs take advantage of the new environment and the opportunities it creates. The great majority of developing countries SME success stories with regard to involvement in e-commerce were largely the result of initial public sector support.

However, while public sector involvement in e-commerce promotion appears to be of critical importance in many cases, it differs in many respects from traditional government interventions. It is more flexible and proactive and relies less on administrative edicts and more on cooperation with the private sector. Rather than maintaining stability, it promotes innovation. The new modus operandi often entails setting up specialized agencies or decentralizing support measures to local governments, for example in countries such as China and India.

To facilitate the implementation of programmes, developing countries need to play a proactive role in encouraging the rapid adoption of market friendly laws and regulations, including laws on e-commerce, electronic contracts and digital signatures. It is equally important to ensure effective coordination of government agencies, industry associations and other facilitators.

At the same time, while e-finance and e-commerce do not eliminate borders, they make them more porous. The Internet may also allow companies and households to circumvent regulations and restrictions. For example, in spite of exchange controls in many developing countries, households and companies still manage to open accounts with foreign banks or brokerage houses via the Internet. The Internet makes the use of offshore companies and banks even easier. The downside is that the Internet offers new opportunities for fraud.

Without a robust regulatory framework, the development of e-finance and e-commerce might be jeopardized. However, if such a framework is too rigid and formal, it may discourage innovation and entrepreneurship and, more importantly, deter the informal sector from engaging in e-commerce. In the end, e-finance and e-commerce will succeed only if they create a stable physical and virtual infrastructure of trust, shared by all parties concerned, including public authorities, local and foreign entrepreneurs, financial services providers and customers, and not the least SMEs.

Creating and maintaining an environment based on trust is essential in order to attract private foreign capital and know-how, as well as financial and technical assistance from international development agencies and NGOs.

Improved tax regimes and simplified regulations, as well as other support measures, will permit SMEs to move towards the formal economy. This will include comprehensive reporting on their assets and liabilities, thus allowing them to be listed in Internet based credit information databases. That might create a fundamental positive change in the financial community's perception of SMEs as credit risks.

In turn, the SMEs will be encouraged to participate in the e-finance revolution and use online banking and payments as part of their common business practices, while as trusted clients they might start to receive online trade finance and eventually investment. This conclusion is valid not only for the overwhelming majority of SMEs in developing countries but also for SMEs in developed countries.

The majority of recommendations of the UNCTAD expert meeting on e-finance for SMEs held in 2001 stressed the role of active policies and public-private cooperation in such vital areas as the creation of an adequate regulatory and institutional environment for e-finance, the development of secure and legally binding methods of electronic transmission and the introduction of modern e-finance instruments.

8

Role of ICTs in Combating Poverty

The fundamental principles underlying a proposed approach to information and communication technologies (ICTs) and development, and draws from those principles a set of recommendations for DFID's priorities in this area. ICTs are defined as technologies that facilitate communication and the processing and transmission of information by electronic means. This definition encompasses the full range of ICTs, from radio and television to telephones (fixed and mobile), computers and the Internet. The role of ICTs in combating poverty and fostering sustainable development has been the subject of increasing debate and experimentation within the international community.

The contrast between the complexity and expense of some of these technologies and the urgent, basic needs of the poor has led some to doubt whether ICTs should be a priority for DFID and other development agencies, or for developing countries themselves. Others have hailed these technologies as holding out great hope for developing countries, and have warned of a growing digital divide between rich and poor that must be narrowed by concerted international action. The study concludes that access to ICTs should not be seen as an end in itself; the measure of success remains progress towards reaching the International Development Targets, rather than the spread of technology or bridging the digital divide.

However, addressing the information and communication needs of the poor and creating information rich societies is an essential part of efforts to tackle poverty. Properly deployed, ICTs have enormous potential as tools to increase information flows and empower poor people.

DFID and other development partners should work closely with developing countries to maximise the contribution of the full range of ICTs to achieving the International Development Targets.

The study recommends that, in its approach to ICT issues, DFID should:

— Mainstream attention to the information and communication aspects of poverty and appropriate use of ICTs in the development process

— Address information and communication issues in national poverty reduction strategies;

— Focus on creating the right enabling environment for the spread of ICTs, for entrepreneurship and innovation, and the free flow of information

— Help the poorest address their information and communication needs;

— Improve and focus the response of the international community;

— Strengthen developing countries' voice in international negotiations on ICT issues.

DFID should build on the progress already made to mainstream consideration of information and communication issues for poverty reduction and the appropriate use of the full range of relevant ICTs as tools in development.

Advisory Departments will need to provide advice and raise awareness in DFID to help staff consider information and communications issues in their work. This process should include providing, for interested staff, concise, evidence-based material drawing on research and experience about what works and what does not.

Advisory Departments are also likely to be the appropriate 'home' for funds for supporting multilateral initiatives related to ICTs. DFID's country and regional departments should consider the recommendations for action with partners in developing countries and determine whether these are priorities for action by DFID in a particular country or region.

Advisory Groups will need to work with staff responsible for interactions with other development agencies to promote greater focus and effectiveness within the international development community. Poverty has multiple and complex causes.

The poor are not just deprived of basic resources. They lack access to information that is vital to their lives and livelihoods: information about market prices for the goods they produce, about health, about the structure and services of public institutions, and about their rights. They lack political visibility and voice in the institutions and power relations that shape their lives. They lack access to knowledge, education and skills development that could improve their livelihoods. They often lack access to markets and institutions, both governmental and societal, that could provide them with needed resources and services.

They lack access to, and information about, income-earning opportunities. These causes are mutually reinforcing. There is a strong correlation between access to education and knowledge, particularly for girls and women, and such key poverty indicators as infant mortality, family size, and women's health.

In poor communities, the scarcity of trained local personnel (teachers, health workers, agricultural extension workers) and the impediments they face in accessing vital information and enhancing their skills, perpetuate the low educational attainment and poor health of these communities and makes them less able to cope with new challenges (such as AIDS, drought, or natural disasters).

These deprivations are compounded at the societal level. Structural impediments to economic growth, and the often highly unequal nature of the growth that does occur in developing countries, perpetuate poverty and inequality. Weak, inefficient or non-transparent markets and societal institutions, including governments, hinder economic growth, deter private sector innovation and investment, and weaken the ability of society to respond to the needs of the poor.

Lack of efficient internal information and communication, even of basic automation of tasks and records, makes government institutions slow and unresponsive, and shifts much of the burden of administrative transactions onto citizens.

Unequal access to, and control of, information creates opportunities for corruption and for the capture of the state by special interests. The poor have information, knowledge and communication needs as do all people, yet they are often unable to address them. Information, knowledge and communication are the lifeblood of economic and social interaction. However, given the multiple constraints they face, the poor are either unable to meet these needs, or must do so in costly ways that may perpetuate their disadvantaged position.

A rural nurse spends a day, and the cost of a bus fare, simply to travel to the regional capital to schedule a training session, for which he or she will have to travel again. A farmer sells goods to middlemen at a low price because of lack of information about prices at market. A mother watches her child die from diarrhoea because she has not learned about oral rehydration therapy. The poor often lack an effective voice in the institutions, policies and processes that shape their lives.

Not only do the challenges of their daily lives often leave poor people little time and opportunity to assert their rights and interests, but they are deprived of instruments for effectively articulating and aggregating their interests, learning about their rights and their entitlements to government services, and pressuring government at all levels to be responsive to their needs and interests. Their lack of effective voice perpetuates inefficient, and sometimes corrupt, forms of governance and service delivery that keep the poor in a subordinate position.

The knowledge and experience of poor people is often undervalued, and their perspectives on their needs and on solutions to their own problems are often ignored. Poor people will benefit from improved information flows throughout society which improve the effectiveness of government, markets and other institutions that affect them.

In societies where information flows widely and access to communication services is widespread, markets and government institutions are likely to become more efficient, transparent and accountable. The institutions and organisations that serve the poor and defend their interests can be more effective.

Information and knowledge that are vital to the poor can be more easily and widely accessible. On the basis of that information, and with tools to communicate with others, the poor can make their own choices, voice their opinions, demand their rights and have more power over their own lives. Increasing communication and the flow of information and knowledge in ways that benefit the poor is therefore a critical component of poverty reduction and sustainable development.

Improving information flows and communication services is a necessary but not sufficient condition to eliminate poverty. The quality, diversity and relevance of information are as important as the sheer volume of information available in a society, or the scale of its communication networks. And even relevant information might not of itself be sufficient. A rural farmer could have the latest crop prices, but still be unable to get a fair price for his or her crop because of unequal power relations with middlemen or poor road networks. Information and communication can be used as tools to exert power over others, encourage violence or perpetuate inequality or prejudice.

While improving information and communication flows, and infrastructures, within a society might foster economic growth at a macro level, the benefits of that growth can be distributed very unequally within society. Therefore, addressing the information and communication needs of the poor must form one important component of a wider strategy to tackle poverty.

Information and communication technologies (ICTs) have an important role to play in reducing poverty by improving flows of information and communications. Much of the recent attention to the role of ICTs in development has focused on new technologies, such as the Internet and mobile phones. Yet the full range of ICTs is relevant to the fight against poverty. Radio and television are important information tools that are much more widespread in developing countries than telephones or the Internet. Print media is vital both to the spread of information and to fostering participation and diversity of views in society. Computers, even if not linked to global networks, are an important tool to increase efficiency in all sectors of society.

New technologies do not change the fundamental role of information and knowledge as drivers of development and poverty reduction, nor obscure the role of more established information and communication technologies. However, they create new opportunities to expand the availability, exchange and impact of information and knowledge.

The potential impact of ICTs on poverty can be seen at the micro, intermediate and macro levels. At the micro level, ICTs can be used by the poor directly to address their information needs, develop their own strategies and solutions for improving their lives, and articulate their interests in societal processes and institutions that affect them.

Properly used and broadly deployed, ICTs can increase the access of the poor to information on market prices for their crops and other goods, to health and educational resources, to information about government services and their own rights as citizens. ICTs can increase the voice and participation of the poor in policymaking, and help them express their needs and priorities to decision-makers. ICTs also enable poor people to share knowledge and seek solutions to their problems.

At the intermediate level, ICTs can help a range of intermediary institutions and agents work more effectively and be more responsive to the needs of the poor. Health workers can access the latest information, get assistance with diagnosis, and more effectively target interventions and resources with the help of ICTs.

Agricultural extension agents can more effectively access and share local and global knowledge on crops, pest management, irrigation and other aspects of small-scale agriculture relevant to the needs of the poorest. Teachers can access and share new training materials, continue their own training, and expose their students to the ideas and experiences of children elsewhere. Local government officials can get better information about the needs of the poor, communicate those needs more effectively to other levels of government, and be held more accountable by the local people they serve. ICTs can help local businesses be more productive, and more responsive to their customers. They can help local non-governmental organisations and community groups to mobilise more effectively, articulate the interests of the poor at the local level and share information and strategies with similar groups elsewhere.

At the macro level, ICTs can help foster more efficient and transparent markets, more participatory processes of governance, and new forms of economic and social innovation that benefit the poor. Broad and efficient information flows, and robust communications infrastructure, are vital components of well-functioning markets.

Weak information flows and poor communications infrastructure constitute one of the major impediments to sustainable economic growth in developing countries. Lack of information, and thus lack of transparency, weaken the responsiveness and accountability of government institutions and create an environment where corruption can flourish. Conversely, when the poor have information about the programmes and resources of government, their rights as citizens, and the match between the declared objectives of government and the actual delivery of services and resources, they have greater opportunities to exert pressure and hold government accountable.

ICTs are a valuable tool for information sharing and awareness raising within the wider development community, to combat poverty and advance the International Development Targets. Multilateral and bilateral development agencies can work more effectively with each other and with their partners in developing countries. A broader range of views and voices from developing countries can be brought into the international debate on poverty and development, including the voices of the poor.

NGOs and civil society groups can network worldwide and collaborate more effectively. Citizens in developed countries can be more effectively exposed to the realities of poverty and the importance of a concerted international response.

There are, however, some limitations and impediments which need to be addressed to ensure that ICTs have a positive impact on poverty. At the macro level, the unequal reach of these new tools and networks could exacerbate inequality.

There is a risk that the rich will have greater access to ICTs than the poor who will be excluded from the benefits of the 'knowledge economy'. This could perpetuate or increase existing disparities of income, knowledge, skills and measures of social development. This heightens the importance of positive measures to meet the information and communication needs of the poorest and assure that these technologies are deployed in a way that expands the information available to the poor, that increases their opportunities for effective voice in the decisions and institutions that affect their lives, and that increases the accountability and transparency of government institutions at all levels.

At the micro level, there are impediments to effective use of ICTs by and for the poor. Some ICTs, such as radio, can be widely accessed without specialist skills except knowledge of the language being spoken. Others, such as use of computers or the Internet, require skills both from users and for the maintenance of decentralised networks and the adaptation of software to local uses. Illiteracy can be a significant impediment to the use of many ICTs (although ICTs can also be used in creative ways to combat illiteracy, such as in the subtitling of television).

Impediments to poor people benefiting from ICTs due to lack of skills can be reduced both by education and training to increase individuals' skills and by developing applications which are adapted to the needs of low skilled or illiterate users.

Poor and disadvantaged groups, particularly women, may face special constraints in accessing ICTs and using them for their specific needs. Women tend to be poorer, face greater social constraints and are less likely to be educated or literate than men. They are likely to use ICTs in different ways, and have different information requirements, to men. Women are less likely to be able to pay for access to ICTs, either because of an absolute lack of funds or because they lack control of household expenditure.

Constraints on women's time or their movement outside of the home can also reduce their ability to access technologies. Similar constraints apply to other population groups who for historical, ethnic or cultural reasons are particularly marginalised or disadvantaged. ICTs are only helpful if users are able to make use of the information and communication opportunities they create.

It is important not only to assure that relevant information is available to the poor in their own languages, but also that ICTs foster the availability of a variety of sources of information, and diverse approaches to the challenges facing the poor, so that they can decide for themselves how to meet their needs. Creating information-rich environments means not only assuring that information is widely available, but assuring that multiple voices (including the voices of the poor and traditionally disadvantaged groups) are heard.

There are barriers to adaptation and innovation of applications of ICTs and content such as broadcast programmes. Radio and television programmes, telephone based information services and computers are all highly adaptable to end users. In the right policy and regulatory environment, people tend to develop specialised products to meet local needs.

However, in many cases, there are barriers to local innovation such as government monopoly of radio broadcasting. Under liberalised broadcasting regimes private broadcasters may be reluctant to invest in producing programming content relevant to poor people because of lack of interest to advertisers.

In some countries, linguistic or other causes of fragmented markets reduces the commercial incentives for production of software applications or radio and television programmes in local languages. The rapid spread of open source software offers considerable potential to reduce the cost of software for users in developing countries and allow greater adaptation of software to needs in developing countries.

Poor people depend on information and knowledge networks that they can trust. Until they come to trust new sources of information poor people may not switch quickly to new technologies even if these allow quicker access to information. This is particularly relevant in countries where information is not freely available and where the media is controlled or heavily influenced by the state or concentrated in the hands of a small elite.

These changes can, in some ways, be helped by ICTs, particularly given their power to bypass or provide alternatives to traditional lines of information and communication. However, the provision of ICTs neither accomplishes by itself, nor removes the need for, those deeper changes.

The impediments to broad deployment of ICTs as tools of poverty reduction are not unique to ICTs as a sector. They are impediments caused by poor governance, inadequate education and training, and poor enabling environments. These are issues that all countries have struggled to address for some time.

ICTs can contribute to addressing these issues, but they do not replace them, and the international community's response to the ICT challenge must be organised in light of this principle. The most important role in creating information-rich environments in developing countries, and making ICTs effective tools for combating poverty and empowering the poor, belongs to developing countries themselves.

Developing country governments need to create enabling environments that will foster the free flow of information, the growth of information and communications networks, the widespread adoption of locally-appropriate ICT tools, and the empowerment of the poor and disadvantaged through the use of these tools and networks. They need to do so in close partnership with their citizens, with the private sector, with civil society, and most importantly with the poor themselves.

In this sense, this challenge is an integral part of the broader challenge of fostering participatory and sustainable approaches to development. A number of developing country governments are already making efforts to realise the development benefits afforded by ICTs, either as engines of economic growth and international competitiveness or as tools of realising the International Development Targets in their country.

An appropriate enabling environment for information and communication technologies, including effective regulatory mechanisms, is essential. Demand for access to information and communication services in developing countries is substantial, even among the poor, and much of this demand is currently not met. There is considerable evidence that the poor are willing to spend some of their resources on information and communications services, if they are available, because they otherwise spend scarce resources (time, money or both) on meeting their information and communications needs in less efficient ways.

Experience from the telecommunications sector around the world suggests that moving from public sector monopoly provision to a well regulated, competitive private market leads to rapid improvements in quality, cost and access to services. Through an appropriate mix of market incentives and government efforts, access can be extended to the poorest and most remote communities. It is equally important that developing country governments implement policies that foster private sector investment and innovation more broadly. For example, small and medium enterprises are a fundamental engine of job creation and economic growth, and they often serve as early adopters of innovation in business technologies and processes. Yet in many countries, there are enormous regulatory and financial barriers to enterprise formation, which hinder innovation and growth.

The economic benefits of improved communication and information flows will be much greater when the enabling environment supports innovation and enterprise creation. In addition, micro, small and medium enterprises are vital providers of many services to poor people, including those related to information and communication.

An effective and dynamic private sector will lead to improved services and cheaper goods for poor people. A third important element of the enabling environment is implementing policies to allow for the free flow of information, and permit and encourage diversity in broadcast and print media. In many countries, restrictive broadcast regimes limit the variety of opinions and information that can be heard by the poor. Governments need to allow and encourage free expression and an independent media with diverse media ownership. For example, making radio licences available for local and community radio stations can increase options for making broadcasting more appropriate to the needs of communities.

Highly concentrated ownership of media outlets can also reduce diversity of information sources and limit the production of local content. Government policies to promote transparency and accountability such as freedom of information legislation can also be important.

Promoting ICT access for the poor, and particularly those in rural and remote areas, requires efforts by government, the private sector, and other partners. The rural poor are typically the last to have access to these services and infrastructures because of technical and economic impediments.

The challenge for developing country governments is to differentiate between those access impediments that could be addressed by private sector or community-led initiatives, given the right policy and regulatory measures, and those that require the commitment of government resources, at least for a transitional period. For example, universal access to telecommunications services—usually defined as access to a payphone within walking distance—is seen by many governments as a public policy goal.

In most countries, the majority of the population can be served on a commercial basis, but government may need to take proactive steps to ensure services are available for the poorest and those in very remote areas.

If the international community is to help developing countries mainstream ICTs as tools of poverty reduction and the International Development Targets, it must organise itself more effectively to do so. This does not mean new ICT initiatives at an international level. On the contrary, it means clarity on objectives, priorities and division of labour. It means focusing ICT efforts on their role in helping to achieve the International Development Targets and not on "bridging digital divides". It means sharing much more effectively and widely the lessons learned from experience thus far.

9

Information Technology and Human Development

People are the real wealth of nations. Development is thus about expanding the choices people have to lead lives that they value. And it is thus about much more than economic growth, which is only a means -if a very important one -of enlarging people's choices. Fundamental to enlarging these choices is building human capabilities -the range of things that people can do or be in life. The most basic capabilities for human development are to lead long and healthy lives, to be knowledgeable, to have access to the resources needed for a decent standard of living and to be able to participate in the life of the community.

Without these, many choices are simply not available, and many opportunities in life remain inaccessible. This way of looking at development, often forgotten in the immediate concern with accumulating commodities and financial wealth, is not new. Philosophers, economists and political leaders have long emphasized human wellbeing as the purpose, the end, of development.

As Aristotle said in ancient Greece, "Wealth is evidently not the good we are seeking, for it is merely useful for the sake of something else." In seeking that something else, human development shares a common vision with human rights. The goal is human freedom. And in pursuing capabilities and realizing rights, this freedom is vital. People must be free to exercise their choices and to participate in decision-making that affects their lives. Human development and human rights are mutually reinforcing, helping to secure the wellbeing and dignity of all people, building self-respect and the respect of others.

Human development challenges remain large in the new millennium. OECD countries more than 130 million people are income poor, 34 million are unemployed, and adult functional illiteracy rates average 15%. The magnitude of these challenges appears daunting. Yet too few people recognize that the impressive gains in the developing world in the past 30 years demonstrate the possibility of eradicating poverty. A child born today can expect to live eight years longer than one born 30 years ago.

Many more people can read and write, with the adult literacy rate having increased from an estimated 47% in 1970 to 73% in 1999. The share of rural families with access to safe water has grown more than fivefold. Many more people can enjoy a decent standard of living, with average incomes in developing countries having almost doubled in real terms between 1975 and 1998, from $1,300 to $2,500.

The basic conditions for achieving human freedoms were transformed in the past 10 years as more than 100 developing and transition countries ended military or one-party rule, opening up political choices. And formal commitment to international standards in human rights has spread dramatically since 1990. These are only some of the indicators of the impressive gains in many aspects of human development. Behind this record of overall progress lies a more complex picture of diverse experiences across countries, regions, groups of people and dimensions of human development.

All regions have made progress in human development in the past 30 years, but advancing at very different paces and achieving very different levels. East Asia and the Pacific has made rapid, sustained progress in most areas, from expanding knowledge to improving survival to raising standards of living.

South Asia and Sub-Saharan Africa lag far behind other regions, with human and income poverty still high. The adult literacy rate in South Asia is still 55% and in Sub-Saharan Africa 60%, well below the developing country average of 73%. Life expectancy at birth in Sub-Saharan Africa is still only 48.8 years, compared with more than 60 in all other regions. And the share of people living on less than $1 a day is as high as 46% in Sub-Saharan Africa and 46% in South Asia, compared with 15% in East Asia and the Pacific and in Latin America.

The Arab States also lag behind in many indicators, but have been making the most rapid progress. Since the early 1970s life expectancy at birth has improved by 14 years and the infant mortality rate by 85 per 1,000 live births, and since 1985 the adult literacy rate has risen by 15 percentage points -faster progress than in any other region.

Differences among regions and countries are particularly marked in economic growth, which generates public resources to invest in education and health services and increases the resources people have to enjoy a decent standard of living and improve many other aspects of their lives.

In 1975 -99 per capita income quadrupled in East Asia and the Pacific, growing 6% a year. The growth rate in South Asia exceeded 2%. Two countries that together account for a third of the world population did well: per capita income in China grew at an impressive 8% a year, and in India at an average rate of 3.2%. OECD countries had average growth of 2% a year, raising already high incomes to an average of more than $22,000 (PPP US$).

But in the Arab States and Latin America and the Caribbean growth has been slower, averaging less thans 1%. Most devastating has been the performance of Sub-Saharan Africa, where already low incomes have fallen; in 1975 -99 GDP per capita growth in the region averaged -1%. Madagascar and Mali now have per capita incomes of $799 and $753-down from $1,258 and $898 (1999 PPP US$) 25 years ago. In 16 other Sub-Saharan countries per capita incomes were also lower in 1999 than in 1975. In Eastern Europe and the Commonwealth of Independent States (CIS) too, incomes have dropped sharply. Since 1990 per capita incomes have declined in 16 countries -in 4 by more than half.

The changing world always brings new challenges, and the past decade has seen serious setbacks and reversals. At the end of 2000 about 36 million people were living with HIV/AIDS -95% of them in developing countries and 70% in Sub-Saharan Africa. More than 5 million became newly infected in 1999 alone.

In Sub-Saharan Africa, mainly because of HIV/AIDS, more than 20 countries experienced drops in life expectancy between 1985 -90 and 1995 -2000. In six countries -Botswana, Burundi, Namibia, Rwanda, Zambia and Zimbabwe -life expectancy declined by more than seven years.

The spread of HIV/AIDS has muitiple consequences for development. It robs countries of people in their prime, and leaves children uncared for. By the end of 1999,13 million children were AIDS orphans. In Eastern Europe and the CIS the disruptive impact of the transition has exacted a heavy toll on human lives, with adverse effects on income, school enrolment and life expectancy, particularly of males.

Personal security continues to be threatened by crime and conflicts. Globalization has created many opportunities for cross-border crime and the rise of multinational crime syndicates and networks. In 1995 the illegal drug trade was estimated at $400 billion, and an estimated 1.8 million women and girls were victims of illegal trafficking.

And because of conflict, the world now has 12 million refugees and 5 million internally displaced people. Democracy is fragile and often suffers reversals. Elected governments have been toppled in such countries as Côte d 'Ivoire and Pakistan.

Human Development Reports, since the first in 1990, have published the human development index (HDI) as a composite measure of human development. Since then three supplementary indices have been developed: the human poverty index (HPI), gender-related development index (GDI) and gender empowerment measure (GEM).

The concept of human development, however, is much broader than the HDI and these supplementary indices. It is impossible to come up with a comprehensive measure -or even a comprehensive set of indicators - because many vital dimensions of human development, such as participation in the life of the community, are not readily quantified.

While simple composite measures can draw attention to the issues quite effectively, these indices are no substitute for full treatment of the rich concerns of the human development perspective.

The HDI measures the overall achievements in a country in three basic dimensions of human development -longevity, knowledge and a decent standard of living. It is measured by life expectancy, educational attainment (adult literacy and combined primary, secondary and tertiary enrolment) and adjusted income per capita in purchasing power parity (PPP) US dollars.

The HDI is a summary, not a comprehensive measure of human development. As a result of refinements in the HDI methodology over time and changes in data series, the HDI should not be compared across editions of the Human Development Report. The search for further methodological and data refinements to the HDI continues.

While the HDI measures overall progress in a country in achieving human development, the human poverty index (HPI) reflects the distribution of progress and measures the backlog of deprivations that still exists.The HPI measures deprivation in the same dimensions of basic human development as the HDI. The HPI-1 measures poverty in developing countries. It focuses on deprivations in three dimensions: longevity, as measured by the probability at birth of not surviving to age 40; knowledge, as measured by the adult illiteracy rate; and overall economic provisioning, public and private, as measured by the percentage of people not using improved water sources and the percentage of children under five who are underweight.

Because human deprivation varies with the social and economic conditions of a community, a separate index, the HPI-2, has been devised to measure human poverty in selected OECD countries, drawing on the greater availability of data. The HPI-2 focuses on deprivation in the same three dimensions as the HPI-1 and one additional one, social exclusion.

The indicators are the probability at birth of not surviving to age 60, the adult functional illiteracy rate, the percentage of people living below the income poverty line (with disposable household income less than 50% of the median) and the long-term unemployment rate (12 months or more).

The gender-related development index (GDI) measures achievements in the same dimensions and using the same indicators as the HDI, but captures inequalities in achievement between women and men. It is simply the HDI adjusted downward for gender inequality. The greater is the gender disparity in basic human development, the lower is a country's GDI compared with its HDI.

The gender empowerment measure (GEM) reveals whether women can take active part in economic and political life. It focuses on participation, measuring gender inequality in key areas of economic and political participation and decision-making. It tracks the percentages of women in parliament, among legislators, senior officials and managers and among professional and technical workers -and the gender disparity in earned income, reflecting economic independence. Differing from the GDI, it exposes inequality in opportunities in selected areas.

In Cambodia in 1999 the HDI for the poorest 20% was 0.445, well below the national average of 0.517 and, more important, nearly one-third less than that for the richest 20%, at 0.623. In Guatemala in 1998 the rural HDI, at 0.536, was well below the urban HDI, at 0.672.

In the United States in 1999 the HDI for white Americans was 0.870, ahead of the 0.805 for African Americans and well ahead of the 0.756 for people of Hispanic origin.

The HDI for untouchables in Nepal, at 0.239 in 1996, was almost half that for Brahmins, at 0.439. Another way to look at the distribution of national achievements in human development is to estimate the human poverty index (HPI), a multidimensional measure of poverty introduced in 1997.

The United Republic of Tanzania and Uganda, for example, have very similar HDI rankings, but Uganda has higher human poverty. Similarly, the 17 OECD countries for which the HPI has been estimated have nearly identical HDIs, yet their HPIs range from 6.8% in Sweden to 15.8%. In the United States. Disaggregating a country's HPI by region can identify concentrations of impoverishment.

In the Islamic Republic of Iran in 1996 the disaggregated HPI showed that human deprivation in Tehran was only a quarter that in Sistan and Baluchestan. The HPI for urban Honduras in 1999 was less than half that for rural areas. For English speakers in Namibia in 1998 the HPI was less than one-ninth that for San speakers. Similar differences exist in the developed world.

Because the HDI assesses only average achievements, it masks gender differences in human development. To reveal these differences, the gender-related development index (GDI), introduced in 1995, adjusts the HDI for inequalities in the achievements of men and women. This year the GDI has been estimated for 146 countries.

With gender equality in human development, the GDI and the HDI would be the same. But for all countries the GDI is lower than the HDI, indicating the presence of gender inequality everywhere. The extent of the inequality varies significantly, however.

For example, while in many countries male and female literacy rates are similar, in 43 countries - including India, Mozambique and Yemen -male rates are at least 15 percentage points higher than female rates. And while there has been good progress in eliminating gender disparities in primary and secondary enrolments, with the ratio of girls to boys in developing countries 89% at the primary level and 89% at the secondary level in 1997, in 27 countries girls 'net enrolment declined at the secondary level between the mid-1980s and 1997.

The gender empowerment measure (GEM), also introduced in 1995, helps to assess gender inequality in economic and political opportunities. The GEM values range from less than 0.300 to more than 0.800, showing the great variation across the world in empowering women. Only 3 of the 64 countries -Iceland, Norway and Sweden -have a GEM of more than 0.800. As many as 25 countries have a GEM of less than 0.500. So, many countries have far to go in extending economic and political opportunities to women.

Some developing countries outperform much richer industrial countries. The Bahamas and Trinidad and Tobago are ahead of Italy and Japan. Barbados has a GEM 30% higher than Greece's. The message: high income is not a prerequisite to creating opportunities for women.

Disaggregations of the GEM in national human development reports show that differences within a country can also be large. For example, the GEM for the Puttalam district in Sri Lanka in 1994 was less than 8% of that for Nuwara Eliya.

There is much to improve in women's economic and political opportunities. Women's share of paid employment in industry and services has increased in most countries, yet in 1997 women working in these sectors typically earned 78% of what men earned.

In only eight countries do women hold 30% or more of the seats in parliament. And in only four -Denmark, Finland, Norway and Sweden -have there been simultaneous achievements in the female secondary enrolment ratio, in women 's share of paid employment in industry and services and in their share of parliamentary seats.

Income is a very important means of enlarging people 's choices and is used in the HDI as a proxy for a decent standard of living. Income growth has varied considerably among countries in recent decades, more so than trends in many human development indicators. The distribution of the world 's income, and the way this is changing, are thus a vital issue deserving special consideration.

Income levels across countries have been both diverging and converging -with some regions closing the income gap and others drifting away.

In 1960 there was a bunching of regions, with East Asia and the Pacific, South Asia, Sub-Saharan Africa and the least developed countries having an average per capita income around 1 /9 to 1 /10 of that in high-income OECD countries. Latin America and the Caribbean fared better, but still had just 1 /3 to 1 /2 of the per capita income of these OECD countries.

The impressive growth in East Asia and the Pacific is reflected in the improvement in the ratio of its income to that of high-income OECD countries, from around 1 / 10 to nearly 1 /5 over 1960 -98. The relative income in Latin America and the Caribbean stayed about the same. Income in South Asia -after worsening in the 1960s and 1970s, then improving significantly in the 1980s and 1990s -remains about 1 /10 of that in OECD countries.

In Sub-Saharan Africa the situation has worsened dramatically: per capita income, around 1 /9 of that in high-income OECD countries in 1960, deteriorated to around 1 /18 by 1998. Despite a reduction in the relative differences between many countries, absolute gaps in per capita income have increased. Even for East Asia and the Pacific, the fastest growing region, the absolute difference in income with high-income OECD countries

For development economists concerned primarily with the world 's poor countries, the central issues have been growth and poverty reduction, not inequality. And for mainstream economists during most of the postwar period of the 20th century, inequality was at worst a necessary evil -helping to enhance growth by concentrating income among the rich, who save and invest more, and by creating incentives for individuals to work hard, innovate and take productive risks.

But income inequality does matter. It matters in itself if people -and nations -care about their relative income status. It may also matter for instrumental reasons -that is, because it affects other outcomes.

Inequality can exacerbate the effects of market and policy failures on growth and thus on progress against poverty. That makes inequality a special problem in poor countries, where imperfect markets and institutional failures are common.

For example, where capital markets are weak, poor people, lacking good collateral, will be unable to borrow. Their potential to start small businesses will be limited - reducing overall growth and limiting opportunities for poor people. Though growth is not always sufficient to advance human development and reduce income poverty, the experiences of China, the Republic of Korea and other countries of East Asia suggest that it makes a big contribution.

Finally, there is the arithmetic reality. Even if there is growth and poor people gain proportionately from that growth, the same growth rate buys less poverty reduction where inequality is high to start with. Concentration of income at the top can undermine the kinds of public policies -such as support for high-quality universal public education -that are likely to advance human development. Populist policies that generate inflation hurt poor people in the long run.

Artificially low prices for water and sanitation mean that bankrupt public utilities never expand to poor neighbourhoods. If rich people support industrial subsidies or cheap loans for large landowners, that may reduce growth directly as well.

Developing and implementing good social policies is especially difficult where inequality takes the form of concentration at the top combined with substantial poverty at the bottom -and thus the absence of a middle class that demands accountable government. Inequality is likely to erode social capital, including the sense of trust and citizen responsibility that is key to the formation and sustainability of sound public institutions.

It can undermine participation in such common spheres of community life as parks, local sports leagues and parent-teacher associations of public schools. Street crime undermines communal life, and differences in income inequality across countries are closely associated with differences in rates of crime and violence.

Inequality may over time increase a society 's tolerance for inequality. If global pressures lead to increases in wage differences (for example, as the salaries of the most skilled and internationally mobile people rise), the social norm for what wage gap is acceptable may eventually shift. If inequality matters for any of the reasons above, the possibility that it can worsen matters too.

Another measure of inequality looks both between and within countries -lining up all the world 's people from richest to poorest (in real purchasing power) regardless of national boundaries. A study by Milanovic compares the poorest and richest people across the globe, giving a much more complete picture of world inequality than a simple comparison of country averages would. Based on house- hold surveys for 1988 -93. The study covers 91 countries and adjusts income levels using purchasing power parity conversions.

The disadvantage is that the study relies entirely on household budget survey data that are not necessarily comparable and are limited in their scope.

Two societies with the same income inequality could differ greatly in the mobility and opportunity facing individual members -and in the mobility and opportunity that children have relative to their parents. A focus on mobility helps to identify the factors that block the opportunities of poor people and contribute to the intergenerational transmission of poverty. This approach is well suited to evaluating the effects of policy changes on poverty and inequality. The problem is that mobility is difficult to measure accurately. Still, the few studies that examine it are suggestive.

In South Africa 63% of households in poverty in 1993 were still there in 1998, while 60% of households in the highest income category in 1993 were still there in 1998, indicating limited income mobility.

In Russia downward mobility was extreme in the late 1990s. Among households in the top income quintile in 1995, nearly 60% slid to lower quintiles by 1998 -and 7% fell to the bottom quintile.

In Peru there has been a great deal of movement up and down the income ladder. Opportunities are increasing with market reforms, but so are insecurities. Between 1985 and 1991, 61% of households had income increases of 30% or more and 14% had income drops of 30% or more. Overall, downward mobility dominated in

The situation is perhaps most serious for under-five mortality. While 66 countries are on track to meet the goal, 83 countries with around 60% of the world 's people are lagging or far behind -and in 10 under-five mortality rates are increasing. While there is not comparable trend data on the prevalence of HIV/AIDS to do a full analysis, the global prevalence of HIV/AIDS among adults is still on the rise, with only a handful of countries, such as Uganda and possibly Zambia, showing signs of decline.

Bibliography

Atkinson, D.; Raboy, M. (eds.). 1997. Public Service Broadcasting: the Challenges of the Twenty-First Century. Reports and Papers on Mass Communication, No. 111. Paris, UNESCO.

Belaud, J.-F. 1997. *The Information Society and European Policies*, Vol. 1. Club de Bruxelles.

Blythe, C. 1997. *The Next Space Race.* Canadian Telecom, Toronto, Ontario.

Brown, M. 1998. *News Consumption in the Internet Age: Audience Shifts That Can't Be Ignored.* Media-info, pp. 10–13. March.

Buckman , R. T. 1996. Current Status of Mass Media in Latin America. In R.R. Cole (ed.), *Communication in Latin America: Journalism, Mass Media and Society,* Jaguar Books on Latin America, No. 14, Wilmington, Delaware, pp. 3–35.

Castells, M. 1997. *The Information Age: Economy, Society and Culture,* Vol. 3: The Power of Identity. Blackwell, Oxford.

Chaum, D. Fiat, A. and Naor, N., "Untraceable Electronic Cash", Proceedings of Cryto 88, 1988.

Feather, J. 1998. *The Information Society: A Study of Continuity and Change.* Second ed. London, LA Publishing.

Hangel J., Sacconaghi, T.M., 1996. "Who will benefit from Virtual Information?" *McKinsey Quarterly,* No. 3, pp. 22–37.

Human Development Report 1998. 1998. New York, UNDP, Oxford University Press.

Konert, B. 1998. "Economics of Convergence, Part 2: The Microsoft Strategy", *Bulletin of the EBU Strategic information Service.* June.

Kubicek H., Dutton W.H., Williams, R., (eds.). 1997. *The Social Shaping of Information Superhighways, European and American Roads to the Information Society.* Frankfurt/New York.

Okamoto, T. and K. Ohta, "Universal Electronic Cash", Proceedings of Crypto 91, 1991.

UNESCO. Sector of Communication, Information and Informatics. On-going Extrabudgetary Projects. Paris, UNESCO, 1998

World Bank. 1998. World Development Report 1997. Oxford University Press.

Index